National Security Agency/Central Security Service

Information
Assurance
Directorate

Spotting the Adversary with Windows Event Log Monitoring

December 16th, 2013
Revision 2

A product of the Network Components and Applications Division

TSA-13-1004-SG

Contents

List of Figures

List of Tables

Disclaimer

This Guide is provided "as is." Any express or implied warranties, including but not limited to, the implied warranties of merchantability and fitness for a particular purpose are disclaimed. In no event shall the United States Government be liable for any direct, indirect, incidental, special, exemplary or consequential damages (including, but not limited to, procurement of substitute goods or services, loss of use, data or profits, or business interruption) however caused and on any theory of liability, whether in contract, strict liability, or tort (including negligence or otherwise) arising in any way out of the use of this Guide, even if advised of the possibility of such damage.

The User of this Guide agrees to hold harmless and indemnify the United States Government, its agents and employees from every claim or liability (whether in tort or in contract), including attorneys' fees, court costs, and expenses, arising in direct consequence of Recipient's use of the item, including, but not limited to, claims or liabilities made for injury to or death of personnel of User or third parties, damage to or destruction of property of User or third parties, and infringement or other violations of intellectual property or technical data rights.

Nothing in this Guide is intended to constitute an endorsement, explicit or implied, by the U.S. Government of any particular manufacturer's product or service.

Trademark Information

This publication has not been authorized, sponsored, or otherwise approved by Microsoft Corporation.

Microsoft®, Windows®, Windows Server®, Windows Vista®, Active Directory®, Windows PowerShell™, AppLocker®, Excel® are either registered trademarks or trademarks of Microsoft Corporation in the United States and other countries.

This publication has not been authorized, sponsored, or otherwise approved by Bluetooth SIG.

Bluetooth® is either registered trademarks or trademarks of Bluetooth SIG in the United States and other countries.

This publication has not been authorized, sponsored, or otherwise approved by USB Implementers Forum, Inc.

USB® is either registered trademarks or trademarks of USB Implementers Forum, Inc. in the United States and other countries.

1   Introduction

It is increasingly difficult to detect malicious activity, which makes it extremely important to monitor and collect log data from as many useful sources as possible. This paper provides an introduction to collecting important Windows workstation event logs and storing them in a central location for easier searching and monitoring of network health.

The focus of this guidance document is to assist United States Government and Department of Defense administrators in configuring central event log collection and recommend a basic set of events to collect on an enterprise network using Group Policy.

This paper focuses on using the built-in tools already available in the Microsoft Windows operating system (OS). Central event log collection requires a Windows Server operating system version 2003 R2 or above. Many commercially available tools exist for central event log collection. Using a Windows Server 2008 R2 or above server version is recommended. There are no additional licensing costs for using the event log collection feature. The cost of using this feature is based on the amount of additional storage hardware needed to support the amount of log data collected. This factor is dependent on the number of workstations within the local log collection network.

Windows includes monitoring and logging capabilities and logs data for many activities occurring within the operating system. The vast number of events which can be logged does not make it easy for an administrator to identify specific important events. This document defines a recommended set of events to collect and review on a frequent basis. The recommended set of events is common to both client and server versions of Windows. Product specific events, such as Microsoft Exchange or Internet Information Services (IIS), are not discussed in this document, but should be centrally collected and reviewed as well.

This guidance document is broken into three main parts. The first part, Deployment, focuses on configuring and deploying central log collection; the second part, Hardening Event Collection, concentrates on security hardening; the last section, Recommended Events to Collect, describes recommended events that should be collected. If a third party commercial product is already being used within an organization to centrally collect events, then skip ahead to the Recommended Events to Collect section. Review the recommended events and ensure they are being collected.

During the development of this guide, testing was conducted using Windows 7 running Windows Remote Management (WinRM) 2.0. A Windows 8 client with WinRM 3.0 was tested as well. Windows Server 2008 R2 was used as the central event collection server. Configuration of Windows Server 2012 should work identically to Windows Server 2008 R2, but was not tested for this guide.

2   Deployment

The Windows Collector service can centrally collect specific events from domain and non-domain computers for viewing on a single computer. The Event Forwarding feature of the Windows Collector Service can retrieve or receive events from remote computers. Event Forwarding can operate as Collector-Initiated (pull) or Source-Initiated (push), respectively. The server archiving the events is a collector and the remote computer, where events are collected from, is the source. A Source-Initiated subscription has an advantage of not requiring the collector to know all the computer names of the remote machines connecting to the service a priori, whereas a Collector-Initiated subscription requires the aforementioned information, which is harder to maintain. The Windows Collector service uses Microsoft's implementation of Web Services-Management (WS-Management, WS-Man) Protocol to communicate between sources and collectors. [1] This guide will discuss configuring event forwarding in domain environments only.

2.1   Ensuring Integrity of Event Logs

Prior to installing and using the WinRM feature, some precautionary measures should be implemented. Although no software can guarantee an attacker could never modify event logs or prevent the recording of event data, an Access Control List (ACL) can be used to protect Windows events logs against accidental tampering.

The Windows operating system uses permissions to ensure that certain log files are not modified by a normal user, members of an unprivileged group or members of a privileged group. The Defense Information Systems Agency (DISA) Security Technical Implementation Guides (STIG) recommends that an Information Assurance Officer (IAO) create an auditor's group and grant members of the group full permissions. If there is no IAO, it is still advised for a system administrator to create an auditor's group. The **Administrators** group's privileges must be reduced from **Full** to **Read** and **Execute** permissions for the Application, System and Security log files. [2] [3] This single defense can be circumvented in multiple ways so; a defense in depth approach should be taken.

This guide does not discuss site specific auditor's group for WinRM purposes beyond this section. The use of WinRM does not require or involve an auditor's group. The auditor's group is used to regulate who is permitted to operate on an event log file. Windows Vista and later created an **Event Log Readers** group whose purpose is to regulate access to the local event logs remotely. [16] [4]

Several domain policies can be enabled to enforce restrictions of users and groups accessing event logs locally. DISA STIGs recommend enabling the **Manage auditing and security log** policy and configuring the policy for the auditor's group. [2] [3] The policy is located under **Computer Configuration > Policies > Windows Settings > Local Policies > User Rights Assignment**. This policy creates a whitelist of users or groups who can access the audit log (security log). Enabling this policy does not affect WinRM operations.

A policy, named **Generate security audits**, can be used to create a whitelist of users or groups permitted to write to the audit log. The policy is located under **Computer Configuration > Policies > Windows Settings > Security Settings > Local Policies > User Rights Assignment**. Only allow Local Service and Network Service as these are the default values of the policy. [2][3]

---

[1] http://technet.microsoft.com/en-us/library/cc774957(v=ws.10).aspx

[2] DISA STIG: Windows Server 2008 R2 Member Server Security Technical Implementation Guide Version 1. Group ID (Vulid): V-1077, V-1137, V-26496, V-26489

[3] DISA STIG: Windows 7 Security Technical Implementation Guide Version 1. Group ID (Vulid): V-1077, V-1137, V-26496, V-26489

[4] http://blogs.technet.com/b/janelewis/archive/2010/04/30/giving-non-administrators-permission-to-read-event-logs-windows-2003-and-windows-2008.aspx

Administrators can use the Enhanced Mitigation Experience Toolkit (EMET) to heighten the security defense of machines and applications used in a network. [5] EMET provides the ability to enable and enforce specific enhanced security features for the operating system and applications. The WinRM service is hosted by svchost.exe (service host). The service host executable should have all security features enabled for an application. Enabling EMET for svchost.exe on Windows 7 does not prevent WinRM from working correctly. Using EMET on a default installation of Windows will not prevent the operating system from performing specific operations. However, site-specific software needs to be first tested with EMET to ensure compatibility.

Recording users or groups accessing event log files (.evtx) is critical and aids in quickly identifying who touched the file. The logging of file access on event log files is not enabled by default and requires additional setup. **Audit File System** policy must be enabled and have **Success** selected to provide useful information. This will allow logging of file system events. The event log file must include the users or groups that will be audited (e.g., **Everyone** or **Domain Users** group) in the **Auditing** tab of the **Advanced** option under **Security** (available in the properties options of the file). Auditing critical files and the operations performed on them increases the value of detecting tampering of the log file.

Using a dedicated server whose primary role is an event collector is recommended. There should be no additional roles tasked to the event collector. Deploying an event collector on a new and clean dedicated system helps protect it from having been previously compromised or infected with malware.

2.2 Environment Requirements

Windows Remote Management is available in multiple versions. The recommended minimal version of WinRM is 2.0. WinRM 2.0 is installed by default with Windows 7 and Windows Server 2008 R2. Additional updates are needed for Windows XP SP3 and Windows Vista to use WinRM 2.0. This guide focuses solely on Windows 7 and above.

WinRM 2.0 is part of the Windows Management Framework core package. The KB968930 [6] update installs PowerShell 2.0 along with WinRM 2.0. This update requires the machine to have .NET Framework 2.0 SP1 or later to install PowerShell. The complete list of applicable Windows operating systems versions and the download location for the updates can be found in the Windows Remote Management Versions section of the appendix. WinRM 3.0 is the latest current version, as of this writing, and is only supported on Windows 7 SP1 and above, Windows Server 2008 R2 SP1, Windows Server 2008 SP2. [7]

This document provides guidance for an environment using three roles in the domain: the domain controller, the event collector, and the event sources. All policies configured through Active Directory are restricted to computer groups, rather than the default Authenticated Users group, for Group Policy Object (GPO) security filtering. The domain controller, collector, and each source in the domain should have the latest updates from Microsoft.

---

[5] https://www.microsoft.com/en-us/download/details.aspx?id=29851
[6] http://support.microsoft.com/kb/KB968930
[7] http://www.microsoft.com/en-us/download/details.aspx?id=34595

2.3 Log Aggregation on Windows Server 2008 R2

A single dedicated server should have the role of event collector in a local network. Isolation of the event collector avoids confusion, frustration of troubleshooting, and security related concerns. Source-Initiated subscriptions can be configured for clients to be in the same or different domain of the collector. The focus of this guidance document is to use Source-Initiated subscriptions, where the collector and sources are in the same domain, and configuring of the event collector is completed locally. Event collector capabilities can be configured via the GPO as well. Utilizing GPO configuration for the event collector will result in the Windows Event Collector service not being properly configured for using subscriptions. Locally configuring the event collector is recommended. The proceeding sections cover local configuration of WinRM and the Windows Event Collection service on the collector.

2.3.1 Locally Configuring Collector Settings

The event collector system needs to be configured to automatically start the Windows Event Collector and Windows Remote Management services. Enabling these services sets the startup type to Automatic (Delay Start). The services will be started after other auto-start services are started plus a short delay. [8] The Windows Remote Management and Windows Event Collector services are automatically configured when using the quickconfig option (discussed in next section). Configuration of the collector can be completed by a domain administrator or a built-in administrator account. The recommendation is to use a domain administrator account for configuration purposes only. It is required that the local administrator and the domain administrator do not have a blank password for WinRM configuration.

2.3.1.1 Enabling Windows Remote Management

The WinRM command-line tool provides an option to automatically configure WinRM. The quick configure (qc) option starts the WinRM service, configures the service to be Delay-Start, creates a listener using any IP address, and enables a firewall exception for WinRM. [9] The port used by WinRM depends on the installed version of WinRM. Port 5985 is used by WinRM 2.0 and above whereas port 80 is used by versions of WinRM prior to 2.0. To configure WinRM, open a command console with administrator privileges and type:

winrm qc

Enter **y** to have the service status changed to Delay-Start. As an alternative option, all prompts can be suppressed by supplying the –q (quiet) option. Enter **y** to the create a listener prompt.

An **Access Denied** error may appear when attempting to use quickconfig. A possible reason for this error is the account executing the WinRM command does not have the proper permissions. If the account is a member of the local administrator group, then User Account Control (UAC) filtering prevents access to the WinRM service. [10] An account with administrator privileges is required. Log in as a Domain Administrator account or a built-in administrator and repeat the quickconfig command.

2.3.1.2 Enabling Windows Event Collector

The Windows Event Collector service offers a quick configure (qc) option similar to WinRM's quick configure option. Windows Event Collector service's quick configure option sets the service startup type

---

[8] http://msdn.microsoft.com/en-us/library/windows/desktop/ms685155(v=vs.85).aspx
[9] winrm qc -?
[10] http://msdn.microsoft.com/en-us/library/aa384423.aspx

to Delay-Start and enables the ForwardedEvents channel. [11] The quick configure option is only available for Windows Vista and above. To configure the Windows Event Collector Service:

wecutil qc

Enter **y** to have the service started and the status changed to Delay-Start. Similar to the WinRM command line, all prompts can be suppressed by the /q:true option.

2.3.1.3 Creating Event Subscriptions

Subscriptions are used to organize event collection and where the events come from. An administrator can have custom subscriptions to tailor event logs to easily identify interesting events. A custom subscription can be created by using the Graphical User Interface (GUI) or from the command line. This section will demonstrate creating an example event subscription to collect events from clients' Application and System logs. It is not recommended to deploy this example on a production server as a large amount of unimportant will be captured. Custom subscriptions provided in this guidance document are discussed in the next section and in the appendix.

The event viewer, shown in Figure 1, allows the configuration of a subscription. Subscriptions can be configured to specify the destination of received events, the computer groups being collected, the event's ID, and the frequency of event collection. Each subscription can be configured in the Subscription Properties window shown in Figure 2. The Event Viewer console should be opened with administrator privileges. To create a subscription:

1. Open **Event Viewer (eventvwr.exe)**
2. Select **Create Subscription...** from the **Actions** panel
3. Provide a **Subscription name**
4. Select the **Source computer initiated** option
5. Select **Computer Groups...** button
   - Click the Add **Domain Computers...** button and enter the group name **EventSource**
   - Click **Check Names** and verify the group name is correct
   - Click **OK**
6. Click **OK**

---

[11] wecutil qc -?

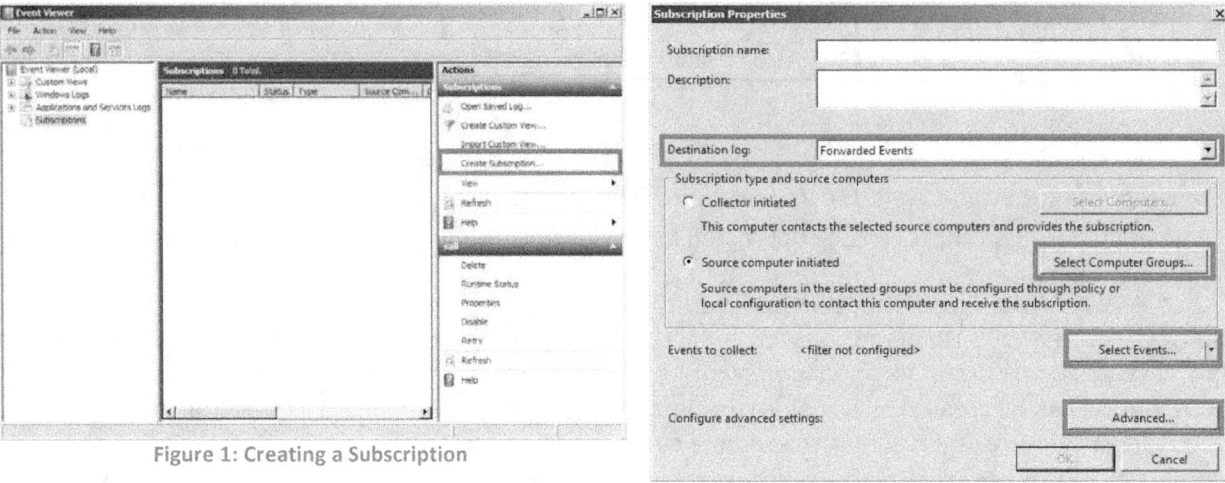

Figure 1: Creating a Subscription

Figure 2: Configuring Subscription Properties

If an error message box appears stating "**the type initializer for 'AdvanceSettings' threw an exception**", then the current account does not have the correct permissions.

Collected Events are stored at a local predefined log location under the **Destination log** drop-down list. The default is **Forwarded Events**.

In the **Query Filter** window, displayed by clicking the **Select Events** button, a variety of events can be chosen for collection based on the event level, origination of log, and event source. Once the setup of filtering events is completed, the XML view of the selected events can be viewed in the **XML** tab. It is possible to edit the XML manually by selecting **Edit query manually** checkbox.

7. Click the **Select Events...** button
8. Select **Event Level** options and select all levels
9. Select **By Log**
10. From the drop-down list select...
    a. **Windows Logs > Application**
    b. **Windows Logs > System**
11. Click the **OK** button

The remaining configuration options do not need to be customized as the default setting will collect all events, keywords, task category, and from all users and computers. Any fine-grained customizations to specify the event to collect are discussed in the next section.

The configuration of advanced subscription settings sets the frequency of events being received (forwarded).

12. Click the **Advanced...** button
13. Select **Normal**
    o Leave the protocol drop-down list set to HTTP
14. Click the **OK** button

6

The Event Delivery Optimization options shown in Figure 3 permits the collection of event logs in 15 minutes (Normal), 6 hours (Minimize Bandwidth), or 30 seconds intervals (Minimize Latency). [12] A custom interval can be set using the wecutil command line utility.

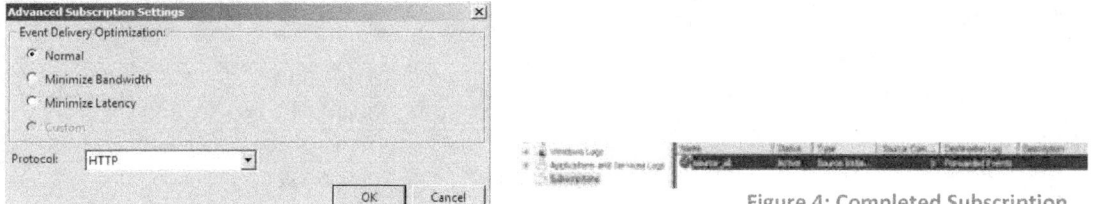

Figure 3: Event Delivery Optimization Configuration

Figure 4: Completed Subscription

2.3.1.3.1 Custom Subscriptions

Creating subscriptions using the graphical user interface does not allow for complete customization. It may be desirable to customize the frequency of event delivery and the batch amount of a subscription (i.e., number of events to deliver per delivery). A detailed description of the subscription schema is found in the Subscription section of the appendix.

Customization of subscriptions depends on the administrator's needs and requirements. Several custom subscriptions have been created and provided in the Subscriptions section of the appendix. These subscriptions collect events that an enterprise may be interested in collecting from domain computers. The following tables summarize the event IDs and the category they represent for each recommended subscriptions. The Recommended Events to Collect section discusses these events in more detail.

Each subscription focuses on varies of categories ranging from account activity, application and computer failures to security notifications and wireless connections.

---

[12] http://technet.microsoft.com/en-us/library/cc749167.aspx

Windows Vista and above Events

General Event Descriptions	General Event IDs
Account and Group Activities	4624, 4625, 4648, 4728, 4732, 4634, 4735,4740, 4756
Application Crashes and Hangs	1000 and 1002
Windows Error Reporting	1001
Blue Screen of Death (BSOD)	1001
Windows Defender Errors	1005, 1006, 1008, 1010, 2001, 2003, 2004, 3002, 5008
Windows Integrity Errors	3001, 3002, 3003, 3004, 3010 and 3023
EMET Crash Logs	1 and 2
Windows Firewall Logs	2004, 2005, 2006, 2009, 2033
MSI Packages Installed	1022 and 1033
Windows Update Installed	2 and 19
Windows Service Manager Errors	7022, 7023, 7024, 7026, 7031, 7032, 7034
Group Policy Errors	1125, 1127, 1129
AppLocker and SRP Logs	865, 866, 867, 868, 882, 8003, 8004, 8006, 8007
Windows Update Errors	20, 24, 25, 31, 34, 35
Hotpatching Error	1009
Kernel Driver and Kernel Driver Signing Errors	5038, 6281, 219
Log Clearing	104 and 1102
Kernel Filter Driver	6
Windows Service Installed	7045
Program Inventory	800, 903, 904, 905, 906, 907, 908
Wireless Activities	8000, 8001, 8002, 8003, 8011, 10000, 10001, 11000, 11001, 11002, 11004, 11005, 11006, 11010, 12011, 12012, 12013
USB Activities	43, 400, 410
Printing Activities	307

Table 1: Vista and above Events

2.3.1.4 Creating Custom Views

Large amounts of event data are difficult to organize and view in a meaningful way. The Event Viewer allows users to create custom views that organize event data based on a custom filter. Each view can be used to represent a subscription to help identify events collected using the subscription. Custom Views were introduced in Windows Vista. [13]

Custom Views can be created on the event collector where all event data is forwarded. To create a custom view:

1. Open Event Viewer and select **Custom Views** in the left panel
2. Right-click and select **Create Custom View...**
3. From the drop-down list titled **Logged**, select a time (e.g., **Last 7 days**)
    a. If a granular time range is needed, select **Custom range ...** from the **Logged** drop-down list
4. Select an appropriate **Event level**
5. Select **By log** and select **Forwarded Events** from the **Event logs** drop-down list
6. Enter **Event ID(s)** in the first text area
7. Click **OK**

---

[13] http://technet.microsoft.com/en-us/magazine/2006.11.eventmanagement.aspx

8. In the **Save Filter to Custom View**, provide a custom view name representing the data being filtered

This creates a custom view under **Custom Views** in the left panel of the Event Viewer. The newly created custom view will not be neatly organized under **Custom Views**. Custom views can be organized by navigating to **%ProgramData%\Microsoft\Event Viewer\Views** and creating a new sub-directory. This newly created directory should have a meaningful name such as "Last 24 hours" to indicate the time period of the events filtered. Creation of the sub-directory requires a privileged account.

To display the new directory when it does not appear after creation under Custom Views:
1. Select **Custom Views** in the left panel of the Event Viewer
2. Select **Refresh** in the right panel

Using a directory named "Last 24 hours," all custom view XML files within the directory should filter events on the condition that the event occurred within the last 24 hours.

An example of a custom view may appear as the following:

```
<ViewerConfig>
 <QueryConfig><QueryParams>
   <Simple>
     <BySource>False</BySource>
     <Channel>ForwardedEvents</Channel>
     <Level>2</Level>
     <RelativeTimeInfo>1</RelativeTimeInfo>
     <EventID>1000</EventID>
   </Simple>
 </QueryParams><QueryNode>
   <Name>AppCrash</Name><QueryList><Query Id="0">
   <Select Path=ForwardedEvents">*[System[(Level=2) and (EventID=1000) and TimeCreated[timediff(@SystemTime) &lt;= 3600000]]]</Select>
   </Query></QueryList></QueryNode>
 </QueryConfig>
</Viewerconfig>
```

The preceding XML looks for events containing EventID 1000 at the Error level (Level 2) that occurred in the last hour (3600000 milliseconds).

The preceding steps focused on automatically creating an XPath query to select event data. This does not allow customization of the XPath queries. Manual XPath queries can be entered in the **XML** tab of the **Create Custom View** dialog.

An alternative option for event filtering is PowerShell's Get-WinEvent and Get-EventLog Cmdlets. These Cmdlets have the added benefit of permitting more granular filtering via other PowerShell Cmdlets.

2.4   Configuring Source Computer Policies
Event forwarding policies can be applied to Windows 7 and above sources with no local configuration. The policies discussed in this section will permit reading of the default log files including the Security log for delivering events to the collector.

2.4.1   Creating Source Group Policy Objects
Following the configuration of the collector it should be in a waiting state to receive events from the sources. The sources are configured similarly with the exception that the Windows Event Collector service does not need to be started and each source needs to be able to read their own event logs. The sources, client computers, will be configured using GP to enable event forwarding. The demonstration below focuses on forwarding events from Domain Computers only.

Each source should be part of a new group and GPO named EventSource where the EventSource GPO applies to the EventSource and Domain Users groups. The EventSource GPO should have both **Enforced** and **Link Enable** settings applied. The members of the EventSource group are domain computer objects. If the machine was powered on when added to the group, then the newly added group member requires a reboot for it to be notified of its membership.

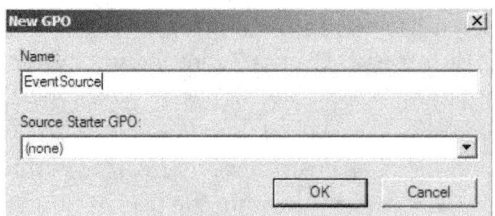

Figure 5: Event Source GPO

2.4.2   Enabling Windows Remote Management Policy

Unlike the approaches used for configuring the collector, WinRM and Event Forwarding will be managed via GP thus not requiring the manual execution of the quick configure option. WinRM can be started using a **System Service** policy. The only issue that may arise is enabling the predefined WinRM firewall rule. Previously, the quick configure option automatically enabled this firewall rule. Active Directory provides predefined WinRM firewall rules to avoid executing the WinRM command manually on all source computers. Configuration of firewall rules is discussed later.

The WinRM service can be found by navigating to **Computer Configuration > Policies > Windows Settings > Security Settings > System Services > Windows Remote Management (WS-Management)** in Group Policy Management Editor.

To set the service to automatic:
1. Right-click the **Windows Remote Management (WS-Management)** service and select **Properties**
2. Select the **Define this policy setting** checkbox
3. Select the **Automatic** option
4. Click the **OK** button

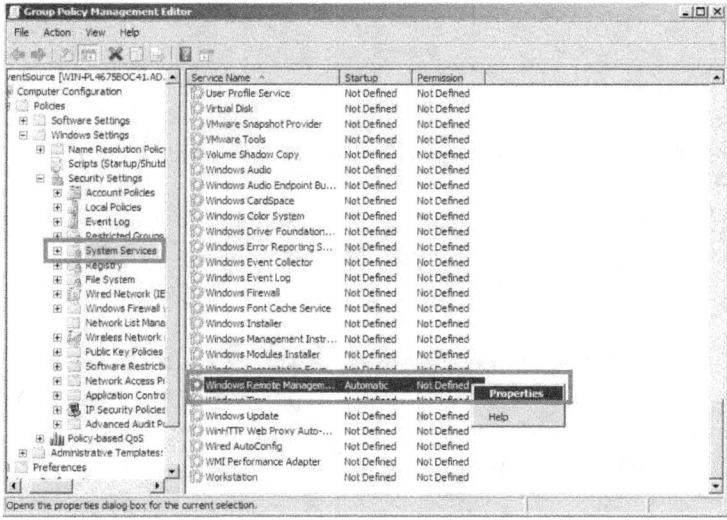

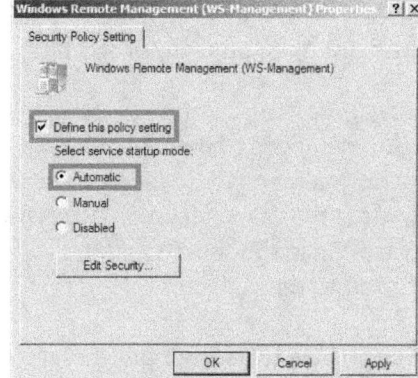

Figure 7: Setting Service Startup Type

Figure 6: Enabling Windows Remote Management

Navigate to the WinRM policies located at **Computer Configuration > Policies > Administrative Templates > Windows Components > Windows Remote Management > WinRM Service** in the Group Policy Management Editor.

WinRM requires listeners to be available for inbound connections. The **Allow automatic configuration of listeners** policy shown in Figure 9 instructs WinRM to create listeners on port 5985 for WinRM 2.0 and above.

To enable WinRM listeners:
1. Set the **Allow automatic configuration of listeners** policy to **Enabled**
2. Set both **IPv4** and **IPv6 filter** value to *

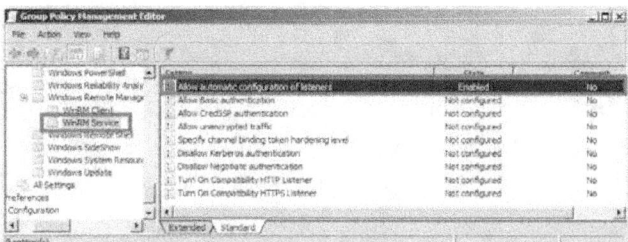

Figure 8: Enabling WinRM listeners

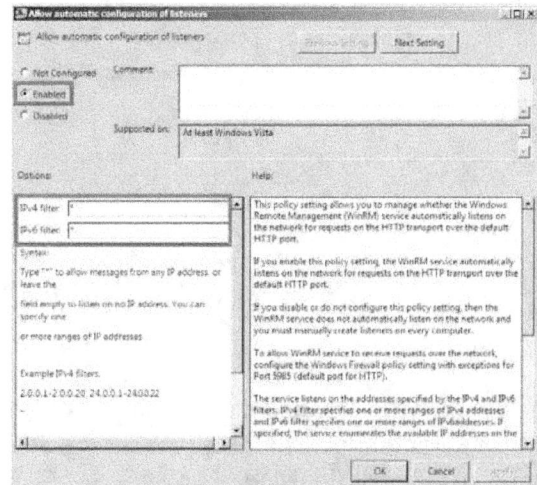

Figure 9: WinRM listener's IP Filter Options

Within the **Allow automatic configurations of listeners** dialog, the **IPv4/IPv6 filter** values should be set to *. This ensures that WinRM starts running and listens on the "any" IP address (IPv4 is 0.0.0.0 and IPv6 is "::") for both protocols. The IPv6 filter is not required to enable a WinRM listener. Enabling an IPv6

11

listener is an administrative decision. The WinRM service only listens on an IPv4 address when no IPv6 address (or *) is supplied for the filter.

2.4.3   Enabling Event Forwarding Policy

The source needs to be configured to forward events to the targeted subscription manager. The subscription manager (collector) hosts all the subscriptions created on the collector. The source needs to contact the manager to retrieve the list of subscriptions. These subscriptions specify the events to forward. Once the source gathers all the events pertaining to these subscriptions, the events will be delivered to the collector.

The **Configure the server address, refresh interval, and issuer certificate authority of a target** policy sets the configuration settings on how to communicate with the collector. This policy sets the collector's internet protocol (IP) address, how often to send events to the collector, and a thumbprint of the client's certificate if using HTTPS. This policy must be enabled to forward events.

Event Forwarding is the main component for enabling event monitoring in an enterprise. Event Forwarding policies can be located by navigating to **Computer Configuration > Policies > Administrative Templates > Windows Components > Event Forwarding**.

To enable Event Forwarding:
1. Set the **Configure the server address, refresh interval, and issuer certificate authority of a target Subscription Manager** policy to **Enabled**
2. Click the **Show...** button

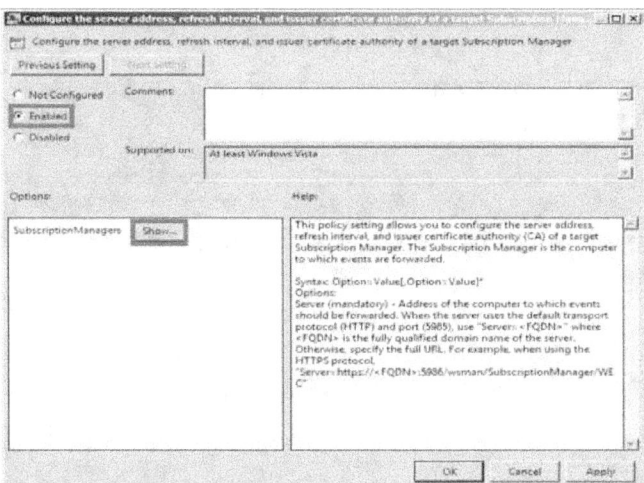

Figure 10: Enable SubscriptionManager

The **SubscriptionManagers** dialog has several options that can be set to configure event forwarding. The only requirement of this policy is to set the **Server** option. Any additional options can be omitted. The syntax of **SubscriptionManagers** value is:

Server=[http|https]://FQDN[:PORT][/wsman/SubscriptionManager/WEC[,Refresh=SECONDS][,IssuerCA=THUMBPRINT]]

Each option for the SubscriptionManager is a comma delimited string containing the following parts:

- Server: FQDN or Hostname
- Refresh: The number of seconds to send events to the server[14]
- IssuerCA: Thumbprint of the client authentication certificate[14]

The last option, IssuerCA, is used for forwarding events between domain and non-domain event collector and sources, respectively. This option can be ignored for our intended purposes. Figure 11 shows an example Subscription Manager value. The refresh interval should be determined by administrative requirements. Using the default refresh interval is recommended.

In a network solely using WinRM 2.0, the **Server** option needs to specify port 5985, otherwise it will send traffic to port 80.

Server=http://FQDN:5985/wsman/SubscriptionManager/WEC

When both WinRM 2.0 and WinRM 1.1 are intermixed and the collector has enabled compatibility mode, remove the explicit port from the Subscription Manager Uniform Resource Locator (URL).

Server=http://FQDN/wsman/SubscriptionManager/WEC

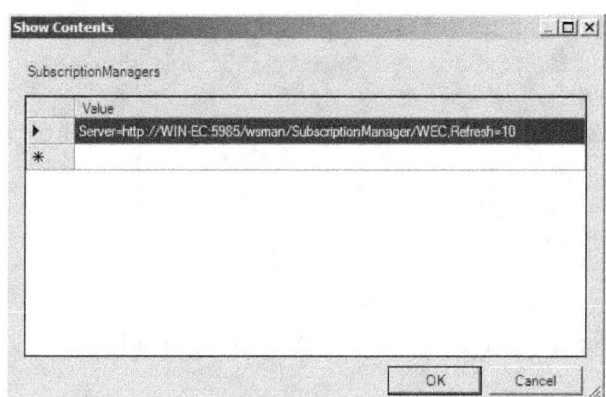

Figure 11: Configuration of SubscriptionManager

Once the **SubscriptionManager** value has been set, click **OK**.

---

[14] http://msdn.microsoft.com/en-us/library/bb870973(VS 85).aspx

WinRM and the Server Option

WinRM will attempt to connect to the collector on port 80 regardless of version. If the URL specified in the **Server** option uses HTTP and has omitted the port value 5985, WinRM will communicate over port 80. The collector may not accept WinRM client connections on port 80 if the latest WinRM versions are used. A compatibility listener can be configured to tell WinRM to additionally listen on port 80. Enabling a compatibility listener on the collector is accomplished by using the following command:

winrm set winrm/config/service @{EnableCompatibilityHttpListener="true"}

The compatibility listener binds WinRM to a second port (80) and accepts traffic on this port. Once a WinRM client has established a connection with the collector, all ensuing traffic will be redirected to port 5985. **EnableCompatibilityHttpListener** intended purpose is to permit versions of WinRM prior to 2.0 to communicate with new versions of WinRM. A caveat to enabling this option is that an additional port will be open on the server, which is a potential security concern. Explicitly specify port 5895 in the URL of the **Server** option when configuring the subscription manager for sources. This avoids the creation of an additional port and firewall rules.

Windows 7 (and above) sources are not permitted to read event logs (e.g., Application, Security, Setup and System) for event forwarding. [15] The sources need to add the **NETWORK SERVICE** account to the **Event Log Readers** group under Restricted Groups in the EventSource GPO. The members of the **Event Log Readers** group are permitted to read event logs. WinRM runs with Network Service permissions on Windows 7 and above. Restricted groups can be configured by navigating to **Computer Configuration > Policies > Windows Settings > Security Settings > Restricted Groups** in Group Policy Management.

To add the **Event Log Readers** to the Restricted Group Policy:
1. Right-click **Restricted Groups**
2. Select **Add Group...**
3. In the **Add Group** dialog box, click the **Browse...** button
4. Enter **Event Log Readers** in the text area of the **Select Groups** dialog box
5. Click **Check Names**
6. Once <u>Event Log Readers</u> appears, click **OK**

To add the Network Service account to the **Event Log Readers** group:
1. Right-click **Event Log Readers** group and select **Properties**
2. In **Event Log Readers Properties**, select **Add...** in the **Members of this group** section
3. Select **Browse...** and enter **NETWORK SERVICE** in the text area
4. Select **Check Names**
5. Once <u>NETWORK SERVICE</u> appears, click **OK**
6. Click **OK** in **Event Log Readers Properties**

The **Network Service** account can be added locally as an alternative option. In Computer Management (compmgmt.msc), add **Network Service** to the **Event Log Readers** group. The **Network Service** account is not part of the **Event Log Readers** group in Computer Management, but can be added by navigating to

---

[15] http://blogs.msdn.com/b/wmi/archive/2009/04/06/forwarding-security-related-events-from-xp-win2k3-vista-using-winrm-wsman-event-forwarding.aspx

Computer Management > Local and User groups > Groups > Event Log Readers and adding this account.

The **Event Log Readers** group will be shown in its SID format (S-1-5-32-573), rather than as an easily readable name, until a Windows Server 2008 or Windows 2008 R2 Domain controller has been made the Primary Domain Controller Operations Master role holder of the domain. [16]

For additional Organizational Units (OUs) that contain user workstations, previously created GPOs can be applied against those OUs.

2.5   Disabling Windows Remote Shell

When WinRM completes execution of quickconfig, Windows Remote Shell (WinRS) will be enabled by default and will accept connections. This poses a security risk as there are attacks that leverage this feature. WinRS should be disabled for all servers and clients in the domain. If the Windows Remote Shell service is needed for a task (e.g., PowerShell's PSSession-family Cmdlets), temporarily enable it and then disable it when the task is completed. The registry keys for WinRS can be found in the WinRM Registry Keys and Values section of the Appendix. WinRS can be disabled for domains via Group Policy. This policy enforcement applies for the collector and sources in the domain.

WinRS policies can be found by navigating to **Computer Configuration > Policies > Administrative Templates > Windows Components > Windows Remote Shell**.

To disable WinRS:
1.   Set the **Allow Remote Shell Access** policy to **Disabled**
2.   Click **OK**

WinRS can also be disabled by using the command line:

winrm set winrm/config/winrs @{AllowRemoteShellAccess="false"}

2.6   Firewall Modification

Event collection aids in identifying problems from a remote computer using WinRM. The communication channel opens an additional attack vector on each of the sources and collectors. The purpose of event forwarding is solely to communicate with the collector(s). An attacker may attempt to attack or perform reconnaissance of other machines laterally with WinRM services. The isolation of sources and collectors limits an attacker from using this service as a target.

Certain environments may enforce firewall rule merging restrictions for servers. Enforcing these restrictions will hinder the configuration of locally applied WinRM firewall rule exceptions. The removal of rule merging restrictions is encouraged for the collection server.

WinRM should have configured Windows Firewall to allow WinRM connections when using quickconfig. The EventSource GPO firewall policies should be enabled for all profiles. This section serves as a list of alternate methods to enable WinRM firewall exceptions. Windows Firewall with Advanced Security policy should be enabled for all profiles.

---

[16] http://support.microsoft.com/kb/243330

2.6.1 Collector Firewall

In Windows Server 2008 R2, Windows Firewall with Advanced Security has two predefined firewall rules that can be enabled from the GUI or the command line. The first predefined rule, **Windows Remote Management (HTTP-In)**, allows network traffic to the local port 5895 on the collector for machines running WinRM 2.0. The second predefined rule, **Windows Remote Management – Compatibility (HTTP-In)**, allows traffic from versions of WinRM prior to 2.0 to communicate with the collector on port 80. The use of the WinRM compatibility firewall rule should be enabled if a compatibility listener is configured on the collector. [17]

WinRM firewall rule must be applied to **Domain, Private,** and **Public** profiles. Any modification of this setting (i.e., selecting **Domain** only) will result in an error with subscriptions running and sources communicating with the subscription manager.

2.6.1.1 Graphical User Interface

Windows Firewall with Advanced Security can be managed using two available options: local or group policies. These graphical options are not required since configuration of the firewall was performed during the WinRM setup and can be used to verify the WinRM firewall rule's status.

2.6.1.1.1 Windows Firewall with Advanced Security Group Policy

The creation of a firewall policy for WinRM can be set using a predefined rule. Expand **Computer Configuration > Policies > Windows Settings > Security Settings > Windows Firewall with Advanced Security > Windows Firewall with Advanced Security – ADsPath > Inbound Rules**.

To enable WinRM firewall rules:
1. Right-click on **Inbound Rules** and select **New Rule...**
2. Select **Windows Remote Management** from the **Predefined** drop-down list
3. Click the **Next** button
4. Select **Windows Remote Management – Compatibility Mode (HTTP-In)** or **Windows Remote Management (HTTP-In)** depending on environment setup. Select both rules if the network is intermixed with WinRM 2.0 and earlier versions.
5. Click the **Next** button
6. Select **Allow the connection**
7. Click **Finish**

The predefined WinRM rule permits either WinRM 2.0 traffic (port 5985) or compatibility mode traffic (port 80). The option to enable the WinRM rule in compatibility mode or not depends if the environment is consist of WinRM 2.0 and earlier versions.

---

[17] See the WinRM and Server Option note of the Enabling Event Forwarding Policy section for more information.

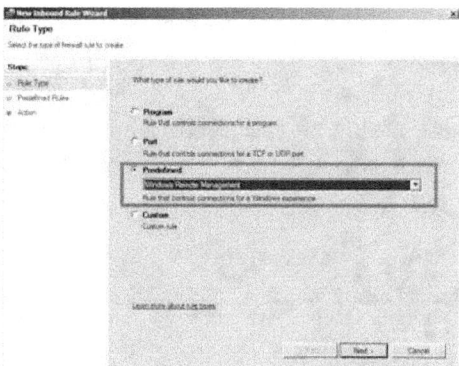

Figure 12: GPO Inbound Firewall Rules

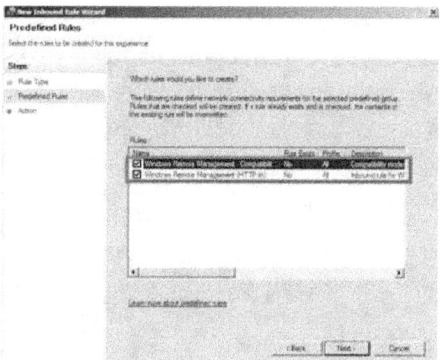

Figure 13: Open Ports for WinRM

The last configuration step for creating the new rule is allowing the connection. Windows Firewall will enable these rules for all profiles and accept traffic from any IP (remote and local) by default.

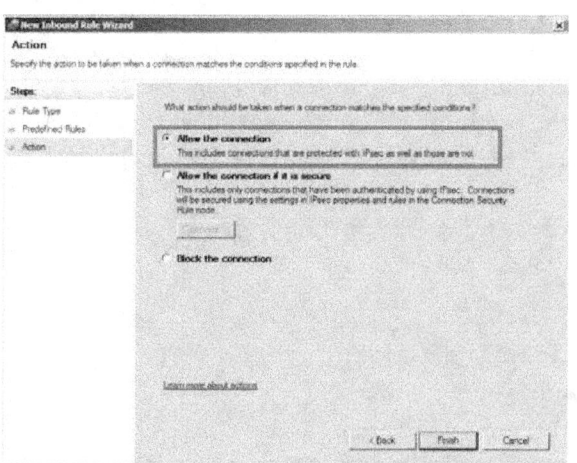

Figure 14: Allow Any Connection to Port

Figure 15: Verify Firewalls are Enabled

2.6.1.2 Configuring the Firewall using the Command Line

The benefit of executing a firewall command allows the user to avoid navigating through the GUI to find the desired configuration options. The following commands demonstrate how to enable WinRM firewall rules for compatibility mode respectively:

netsh advfirewall firewall set rule name="Windows Remote Management (HTTP-In)" new enable=yes

If an error message "A specific value is not valid" appears, verify the rule's name. The alternative approach is to enter the netsh context, followed by the advfirewall context, and the firewall context. In the firewall context, repeat the command for the specific rule.

2.6.2 WinRM 2.0 Source Firewall

When WinRM is executed with the quickconfig option, it creates a default firewall rule that allows inbound WinRM traffic. The firewall rule automatically sets the required port (80 or 5985) depending on the WinRM version. Configuring WinRM locally on sources is discouraged as using Group Policy is more manageable.

Sources using WinRM 2.0 require that port 5985 is allowed through the firewall. The predefined rule **Windows Remote Management (HTTP-In)** should only be enabled on a computer using WinRM 2.0. The steps for enabling the firewall rule via GPO for the sources can be done by following the Windows Firewall with Advanced Security Group Policy section. This rule should be applied to Windows Vista (if upgraded to WinRM 2.0) and beyond as it uses Windows Firewall with Advanced Security. The firewall rule should be applied to **Domain** profiles only.

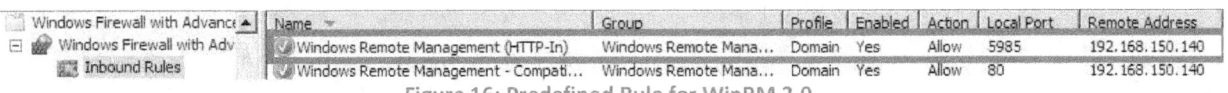

Name	Group	Profile	Enabled	Action	Local Port	Remote Address
Windows Remote Management (HTTP-In)	Windows Remote Mana...	Domain	Yes	Allow	5985	192.168.150.140
Windows Remote Management - Compati...	Windows Remote Mana...	Domain	Yes	Allow	80	192.168.150.140

Figure 16: Predefined Rule for WinRM 2.0

Once the WinRM firewall rule is enabled, update the group policy changes using gpupdate. Events should be populating the collector's log. If no events are received, then troubleshooting techniques are provided in the Troubleshooting section.

2.7   Restricting WinRM Access

The default rules permit connections from any IP address to the specific WinRM port. An attacker who has presence on a network can possibly move laterally between machines and servers by accessing WinRM services. Mitigation to this attack is customizing the predefined rules to only allow connections between collectors and sources. A policy for specifying the IP scope for both source and collector machine is discussed in this section. These configurations apply to the WinRM predefined firewall rules under **Computer Configuration > Policies > Windows Settings > Security Settings > Windows Firewall with Advanced Security > Inbound Rules**.

2.7.1   Source Firewall Modifications

To enable WinRM firewall rules on the sources:
1. Right-click the predefined WinRM firewall rule and select **Properties**
2. Navigate to the **Scope** tab
3. In the **Remote IP Address** area and select the **These IP addresses** option
4. Click the **Add...** button
5. Select the **This IP address or subnet** option and enter the IP address of the collector
6. Click **OK**

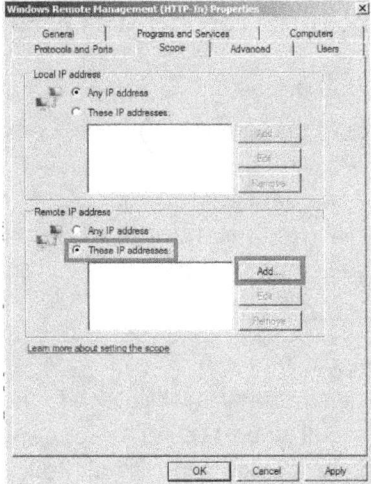

Figure 17: Adding Selective IP addresses

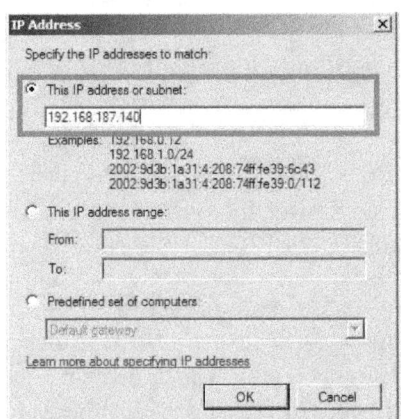

Figure 18: Add IP of Event Collector

Configuring a whitelist, which accepts WinRM traffic only from the collector, is recommended.

2.7.2   Collector Firewall Modification

As done in the Source Firewall Modifications section, repeat the steps for the predefined WinRM rule. Setting the **Predefined set of computers** option to **Local subnet** is recommended. This rule can be changed to best suit your environment.

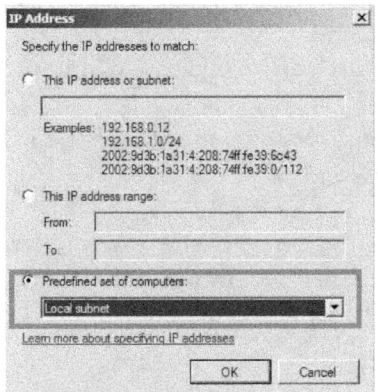

Figure 19: The Event Collector Firewall allowing Local subnet to Connect

---

Group Policy Firewall Problem

While viewing a subscription in Event Viewer, the following error *may* appear. As the dialog states, a firewall exception needs to be applied or a firewall setting was modified incorrectly. Verify that when you enabled the predefined firewall rules via a Group Policy that the firewall profile for the rule is enabled as well. A more detailed error message can be obtained by providing the name of the desired subscription (subscriptionID):

wecutil get-subscriptionruntimestatus *SubscriptionID*

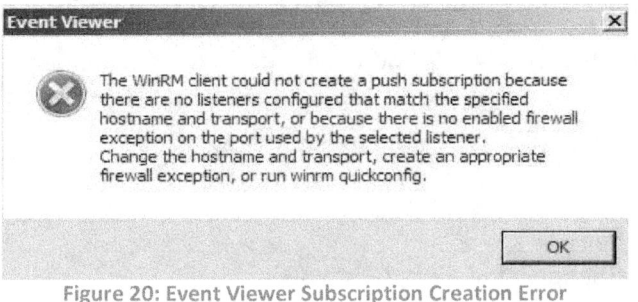

Figure 20: Event Viewer Subscription Creation Error

2.8   Disabling WinRM and Windows Collector Service

Windows Remote Management (WinRM) and Event Forwarding can be disabled from operating in the network. These services can be stopped in the Services Microsoft Management Console (MMC) snap-in. Each subscription created and in use should be disabled on the event collector server.

To disable collection of events on the event collector server:
1. Open **Services** MMC snap-in
2. Right-click the **Windows Remote Management** service and select **Properties**
3. Change the **Startup type** to **Disabled**

4. In Services status option, select **Stop**
5. Click **OK**
6. Repeat steps 1 through 5 for the **Windows Event Collector** service

WinRM can be disabled on each source that was configured by a GP. The following steps are performed on the Domain Controller for domains using WinRM and Event Forwarding:

1. Open Group Policy Management Editor
2. Navigate to **Computer Configuration > Policies > Windows Settings > Security Settings > System Services**
3. Right-click the **Windows Remote Management** service and select **Properties**
4. Set **Startup** type to **Disabled**
5. Click **OK**
6. Navigate to **Computer Configuration > Policies > Administrative Templates > Event Forwarding**
7. Set the **Configure the server address, refresh interval, and issuer certificate authority of a target Subscription Manager** policy to **Disabled**
8. Click **OK**

Repeat the above steps for any additional OUs that use Event Forwarding and WinRM.

3 Hardening Event Collection

Windows Remote Management (WinRM) provides security options for authentication and uses other security technologies to encrypt communication channels. This section explains how to securely configure WinRM.

3.1 WinRM Authentication Hardening Methods

WinRM configuration is divided into two parts: service and client. The service configuration is used to manage the WinRM service that receives WS-Management requests from clients. [18]

The following methods of authentication are supported by WinRM: [19]

- Basic Authentication
- Digest Authentication
- Credential Security Support Provider (CredSSP)
- Negotiate Authentication
- Kerberos Authentication
- Client Certificate-based Authentication
- Channel Binding Token

The authentication methods for the WinRM client and service can be located by navigating to **Computer Configuration > Policies > Administrative Templates > Windows Components > Windows Remote Management (WinRM)**. WinRM Service and WinRM Client authentication methods are respectively shown in Figure 21 and Figure 22.

---

[18] http://technet.microsoft.com/en-us/library/cc775103(v=ws.10).aspx
[19] http://msdn.microsoft.com/en-us/library/windows/desktop/aa384372(v=vs.85).apsx

The client has the option to set Digest Authentication, while the service does not. Additionally, the service can allow hardening of WinRM TLS connections using channel binding tokens.

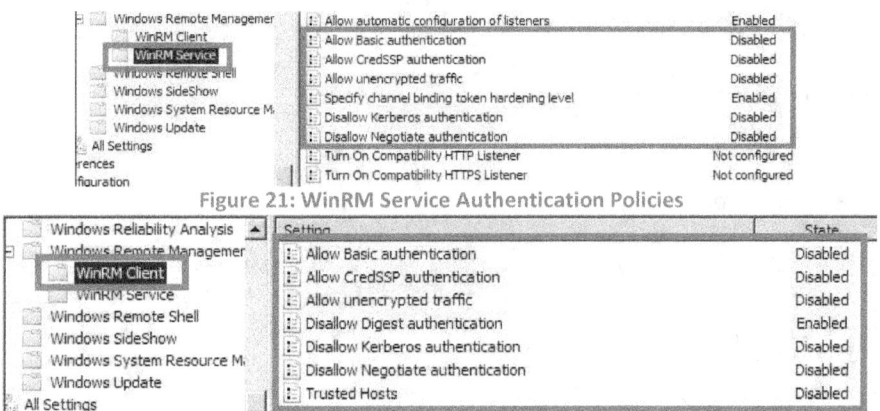

Figure 21: WinRM Service Authentication Policies

Figure 22: WinRM Client Authentication Policies

The **Allow unencrypted traffic** policy is not part of authentication. Default value for both Client and Service configuration of the aforementioned policy is **Disabled**. Setting this policy to **Disabled** is recommended.

3.1.1 Basic Authentication

The client can use basic authentication to communicate with a WinRM service. Setting the **Allow Basic authentication** to **Disabled** is recommended.

Default Client Configuration: **True**
Default Service Configuration: **False**

Setting both to **Disabled** is recommended.

3.1.2 Digest Authentication

This mode of authentication is a challenge-response scheme. The client will initiate the request and in response, the server will send a server-specified token string to the client. After the token string has been received, the client will append the resource request with the username of the client, the hash of the username's password, and the token string to the response message. [19]

The WinRM service does not accept digest authentication as shown in Figure 21. [20][21]

Default Service Configuration: **Not Applicable**
Default Client Configuration: **True**

Setting the client configuration to **False** is recommended.

Setting the **Disallow Digest Authentication** policy to **Enabled** is recommended.

---

[20] http://msdn.microsoft.com/en-us/library/windows/desktop/aa384295(v=vs.85).aspx
[21] http://msdn.microsoft.com/en-us/library/windows/desktop/aa384372(v=vs.85).aspx

3.1.3 Credential Security Support Provider

Credential Security Support Provider (CredSSP) provides a secure way to delegate a user's credentials from a client to a target server. [19][22][23] The SSP provides the capability of Single Sign-on (SSO) in Terminal Services sessions. [23] This option is only available for WinRM 2.0. Setting the **Allow CredSSP authentication policy** to **Disabled** is recommended.

Default Client Configuration: **False**
Default Service Configuration: **False**

Setting both to **Disabled** is recommended.

3.1.4 Negotiate Authentication

Negotiate authentication is a Security Support Provider (SSP) that provides a client two alternative methods for authentication: Kerberos and NTLM. [24][25][26] Negotiate will initially select Kerberos as the default; otherwise, NTLM is used. [19]

Default Client Configuration: **True**
Default Service Configuration: **True**

Disabling Negotiate authentication may result in unforeseen problems when trying to configure WinRM locally. It is recommended to complete configuration of the event collection network prior to enforcing this policy. Issuing the WinRM command with the remote destination switch containing the local host value while the client machine is part of a domain, WinRM will use Negotiate authentication. [27] If an error arises stating Negotiate authentication is disabled, a workaround is to use Kerberos locally by specifying the local hostname in the remote switch. [28] Setting the **Disallow Negotiate Authentication** policy to **Enabled** is recommended.

Setting both to **Enabled** is recommended.

3.1.5 Kerberos Authentication

Kerberos version 5 is used as a method of authentication and communication between the service and client. [29][30][31] Setting the **Disallow Kerberos Authentication** policy to **Disabled** is recommended.

Default Client Configuration: **True**
Default Service Configuration: **True**

Setting both to **Disabled** is recommended.

---

22 ([MS-CSSP]: Credential Security Support Provider (CredSSP) Procotol, 2012)
23 http://technet.microsoft.com/en-us/library/cc749211(WS.10).aspx
24 http://technet.microsoft.com/en-us/library/cc755084(v=ws.10).aspx
25 (Installation and Configuration for Windows Remote Management, 2012)
26 http://msdn.microsoft.com/en-us/library/windows/desktop/aa378748(v=vs.85).aspx
27 http://msdn.microsoft.com/en-us/library/windows/desktop/aa384295(v=vs.85).aspx
28 WinRM errorcode 0x803380E1
29 http://www.ietf.org/rfc/rfc1510.txt
30 http://technet.microsoft.com/en-us/library/cc772815(v=ws.10).aspx
31 http://technet.microsoft.com/en-us/library/cc753173(v=ws.10).aspx

3.1.6   Client Certificate-Based Authentication

Services can verify the connecting client's authenticity by examining its certificate. If the authentication process fails, then the client's connection is rejected.

Default Client Configuration: **True**
Default Service Configuration: **False**

Setting both to **False** is recommended.

There is no Group Policy setting to disable Certificate-Based Authentication for WinRM's client configuration. The only alternative is via the command line:

> **winrm set winrm/config/client/auth @{Certificate="false"}**[32]

Accessing each source to manually configure this setting is not recommended. This authentication recommendation should be set on the collector.

3.1.7   Channel Binding Token

A common threat amongst NTLM, NTLMv2, and Kerberos authentication methods is a Man-in-the-Middle (MitM) attack. [33] Channel Binding Token (CBT) authentication option involves securing communication channels between a client and server using Transport Layer Security (TLS). A MitM attacker is positioned between a client and a server to impersonate as both the server and client. When the client initiates a request to the server, the attacker captures the client's first request and forwards it to the server on the client's behalf. The server responds with an authentication request. The attacker receives the server's request and forwards the request to the client. When this request is received by the client, the client sends their credentials as a response. As previously done, these credentials are sent to the attacker because the client assumes it is communicating with the server and now the attacker can access the resource. [34][35][36]

CBT improves the security of the communication channel between the server and the client. If a MitM is being conducted, then the two connections will generate two different tokens (sessions in particular; server-to-attacker and client-to-attacker). When the CBT-aware server notices this discrepancy, it will refuse the authentication request. Note, **this option is not available prior to WinRM 2.0**.

Channel Binding Tokens option can be set to: [37]
* **None** - Not using any CBTs
* **Relaxed** - Any invalid tokens are rejected, but any channel without a binding token will be accepted
* **Strict** - Any request with an invalid channel token is rejected

Default Service Configuration: **Relaxed**

---

[32] If you get an error regarding Negotiate authentication failed after applying hardening authentication methods, see Troubleshooting section in Appendix and the Negotiate Authentication section.

[33] Securing Windows Networks: Security Advice From The Front Line by Robert Hensing – Microsoft PSS Security; http://it.northwestern.edu/bin/docs/windows_network.ppt

[34] http://msdn/microsoft.com/en-us/library/vstudio/dd767318(v=vs.90).aspx

[35] http://blogs.technet.com/b/srd/archive/2009/12/08/extended-protection-for-authentication.aspx

[36] http://tools.ietf.org/html/rfc5056

[37] **Specify channel binding token hardening level** policy within **Windows Remote Management > WinRM Service** on Windows Server 2008 R2.

If using TLS, setting the **Specify channel binding token hardening level** policy to **Strict** is recommended; otherwise, set the policy to **Disabled**.

3.1.8   Trusted Host

Trusted Host authentication is used for computers not using HTTPS or Kerberos for authentication. [38] A list of computers (non-domain members) can be provided and marked trusted. These computers, when using WinRM, will not be authenticated. [21]

Default Client Configuration: **False**

Setting the **Trusted Hosts** policy to **Disabled** is recommended unless collection from non-domain sources required.

3.2   Secure Sockets Layer and WinRM

Event Forwarding is not solely for domain joined computers. Computers not joined to a domain can use the Event Forwarding feature of Windows under the condition that TLS/SSL is used. WinRM traffic between the collector and source, domain or non-domain computers, are encrypted either using Windows Integrated Authentication or HTTPS respectively. [20][39][90] The message payload of WinRM's HTTP traffic is encrypted using one of the three authentication methods provided by Integrated Windows Authentication: Negotiate, Kerberos, or CredSSP. [40][41][83] The default encryption method used for WinRM's HTTP traffic is Kerberos or Negotiate; otherwise TLS/SSL is used. [42][43] WinRM for non-domain computer uses client certificate mapping to authenticate the collector and source. The general steps consist of configuring the listening port, creating certificates for collectors and sources, configuring the subscription manager, creating certificates, and configuring subscriptions. A more detailed explanation of configuring WinRM to use TLS/SSL for non-domain computers is provided by Microsoft. [14][43]

4   Recommended Events to Collect

This section contains a basic set of events recommended for central collection and review by administrators. The presence of a collected event is not necessarily malicious, and should be reviewed in the appropriate context. Event logs provide a record of activities that can be referenced when malicious activity is discovered on a workstation. Microsoft has released a document titled **Best Practices for Securing Active Directory** [44] focusing on several topics from defending against different attacks on Active Directory installations to recommending an extensive list of events to monitor in a domain. The events recommended herein are critical to identify behavior and health of a machine.

Collection of the certain recommended events (e.g., account logons) require Domain Controllers or Member servers to be configured for Event Forwarding as a source. Certain events (e.g., account

---

[38] http://technet.microsoft.com/en-us/magazine/ff700227.aspx
[39] http://support.microsoft.com/kb/2019527
[40] http://msdn.microsoft.com/en-us/library/cc251574.aspx
[41] http://technet.microsoft.com/en-us/security/advisory/974926
[42] winrm help config
[43] http://support.microsoft.com/kb/2019527
[44] http://www.microsoft.com/en-us/download/details.aspx?id=38785

management) are only generated on Domain Controllers in a domain setting whereas those same events are generated on the local machine in non-domain settings.

4.1 Application Whitelisting

Application whitelisting events should be collected to look for applications that have been blocked from execution. Any blocked applications could be malware or users trying to run unapproved software. Software Restriction Policies (SRP) is supported on Windows XP and above. The AppLocker feature is available for Windows 7 and above Enterprise and Ultimate editions only. [45] Application Whitelisting events can be collected if SRP or AppLocker are actively being used on the network.

	ID	Level	Event Log	Event Source
AppLocker Block	8003 8004	Error Warning	Microsoft-Windows-AppLocker/EXE and DLL	Microsoft-Windows-AppLocker
AppLocker Warning	8006 8007	Error Warning	Microsoft-Windows-AppLocker/MSI and Script	Microsoft-Windows-AppLocker
SRP Block	865, 866, 867, 868, 882	Warning	Application	Microsoft-Windows-SoftwareRestrictionPolices

Table 2: Whilelisting Events

4.2 Application Crashes

Application crashes may warrant investigation to determine if the crash is malicious or benign. Categories of crashes include Blue Screen of Death (BSOD), Windows Error Reporting (WER), Application Crash and Application Hang events. If the organization is actively using the Microsoft Enhanced Mitigation Experience Toolkit (EMET), then EMET logs can also be collected.

	ID	Level	Event Log	Event Source
App Error	1000	Error	Application	Application Error
App Hang	1002	Error	Application	Application Hang
BSOD	1001	Error	System	Microsoft-Windows-WER-SystemErrorReporting
WER	1001	Informational	Application	Windows Error Reporting
EMET	1 2	Warning Error	Application Application	EMET

Table 3: Application Events

4.3 System or Service Failures

System and Services failures are interesting events that may need to be investigated. Service operations normally do not fail. If a service fails, then it may be of concern and should be reviewed by an administrator. If a Windows service continues to fail repeatedly on the same machines, then this may indicate that an attacker is targeting a service.

	ID	Level	Event Log	Event Source
Windows Service Fails or Crashes	7022, 7023, 7024, 7026, 7031, 7032, 7034	Error	System	Service Control Manager

Table 4: System Events

---

[45] http://technet.microsoft.com/en-us/library/dd759131.aspx

4.4 Windows Update Errors

A machine must be kept up to date to mitigate known vulnerabilities. Although unlikely, these patches may sometimes fail to apply. Failure to update issues should be addressed to avoid prolonging the existence of an application issue or a vulnerability in the operating system or an application.

	ID	Level	Event Log	Event Source
Windows Update Failed	20, 24, 25, 31, 34, 35	Error	Microsoft-Windows-WindowsUpdateClient/Operational	Microsoft-Windows-WindowsUpdateClient
Hotpatching Failed	1009	Informational	Setup	Microsoft-Windows-Servicing

Table 5: Windows Update Failed Events

4.5 Windows Firewall

If client workstations are taking advantage of the built-in host-based Windows Firewall, then there is value in collecting events to track the firewall status. For example, if the firewall state changes from on to off, then that log should be collected. Normal users should not be modifying the firewall rules of their local machine.

	ID	Level	Event Log	Event Source
Firewall Rule Add	2004	Informational	Microsoft-Windows-Windows Firewall With Advanced Security/Firewall	Microsoft-Windows-Windows Firewall With Advanced Security
Firewall Rule Change	2005	Informational	Microsoft-Windows-Windows Firewall With Advanced Security/Firewall	Microsoft-Windows-Windows Firewall With Advanced Security
Firewall Rules Deleted	2006, 2033	Informational	Microsoft-Windows-Windows Firewall With Advanced Security/Firewall	Microsoft-Windows-Windows Firewall With Advanced Security
Firewall Failed to load Group Policy	2009	Error	Microsoft-Windows-Windows Firewall With Advanced Security/Firewall	Microsoft-Windows-Windows Firewall With Advanced Security

Table 6: Firewall Events

The above events for the listed versions of the Windows operating system are only applicable to modifications of the local firewall settings.

4.6 Clearing Event Logs

It is unlikely that event log data would be cleared during normal operations and it is likely that a malicious attacker may try to cover their tracks by clearing an event log. When an event log gets cleared, it is suspicious. Centrally collecting events has the added benefit of making it much harder for an attacker to cover their tracks. Event Forwarding permits sources to forward multiple copies of a collected event to multiple collectors thus enabling redundant event collection. Using a redundant event collection model can minimize the single point of failure risk.

	ID	Level	Event Log	Event Source
Event Log was Cleared	104	Informational	System	Microsoft-Windows-Eventlog
Audit Log was Cleared	1102	Informational	Security	Microsoft-Windows-Eventlog

Table 7: Log Activity Events

4.7 Software and Service Installation

As part of normal network operations, new software and services will be installed, and there is value in monitoring this activity. Administrators can review these logs for newly installed software or system services and verify that they do not pose a risk to the network.

	ID	Level	Event Log	Event Source
New Kernel Filter Driver	6	Informational	System	Microsoft-Windows-FilterManager
New Windows Service	7045	Informational	System	Service Control Manager
New MSI File Installed	1022, 1033	Informational	Application	MsiInstaller
New Application Installation	903, 904[46]	Informational	Microsoft-Windows-Application-Experience/Program-Inventory[47]	Microsoft-Windows-Application-Experience
Updated Application	905, 906[46]	Informational	Microsoft-Windows-Application-Experience/Program-Inventory	Microsoft-Windows-Application-Experience
Removed Application	907, 908[46]	Informational	Microsoft-Windows-Application-Experience/Program-Inventory	Microsoft-Windows-Application-Experience
Summary of Software Activities	800	Informational	Microsoft-Windows-Application-Experience/Program-Inventory	Microsoft-Windows-Application-Experience
Update Packages Installed	2	Informational	Setup	Microsoft-Windows-Servicing
Windows Update Installed	19	Informational	System	Microsoft-Windows-WindowsUpdateClient

Table 8: Software and Service Events

It should be noted that an additional Program Inventory event ID 800 is generated, on Windows 7, daily at 12:30 AM to provide a summary of application activities (e.g., numbers of new application installation).[48] Event ID 800 is generated on Windows 8 as well under different circumstances. This event is beneficial to administrators seeking to identify the number of applications were installed or removed on a machine.

4.7.1 Program Data Updater

Administrators may have a process of inventorying software installed on clients. Windows has a component, Application-Experience, which tracks the activities of adding and removing software.

The Program-Inventory log file is used by a scheduled task called Program Data Updater under **Microsoft > Windows > Application Experience** of the Task Scheduler. Program Data Updater is described as an application that "collects program telemetry information if opted-in to the Microsoft Customer Experience Improvement Program."[49] It is not required to be opted-in to the Microsoft Customer Experience Improvement Program (CEIP) to generate event ID 800, 903, 904, 905, 906, 907, or 908.

These events do not apply to standalone executables.

4.8 Account Usage

User account information can be collected and audited. Tracking local account usage can help detect Pass the Hash activity and other unauthorized account usage. Additional information such as remote desktop logins, users added to privileged groups, and account lockouts can also be tracked. User

---

[46] These events only apply to Windows 7 as they were removed in Windows 8+.
[47] Full Log Path is **Applications and Services Logs > Microsoft > Windows > Application-Experience > Program-Inventory**
[48] Trigger information for Application Experience was taken from ProgramDataUpdater scheduled task
[49] This description can be found under the **General** tab of the task called **ProgramDataUpdater**.

accounts being promoted to privileged groups should be audited very closely to ensure that users are in fact supposed to be in a privileged group. Unauthorized membership in privileged groups is a strong indicator that malicious activity has occurred.

	ID	Level	Event Log	Event Source
Account Lockouts	4740	Informational	Security	Microsoft-Windows-Security-Auditing
User Added to Privileged Group	4728, 4732, 4756	Informational	Security	Microsoft-Windows-Security-Auditing
Security-Enabled group Modification	4735	Informational	Security	Microsoft-Windows-Security-Auditing
Successful User Account Login	4624	Informational	Security	Microsoft-Windows-Security-Auditing
Failed User Account Login	4625	Informational	Security	Microsoft-Windows-Security-Auditing
Account Login with Explicit Credentials	4648	Informational	Security	Microsoft-Windows-Security-Auditing

Table 9: Account Activity Events

Lockout events for domain accounts are generated on the domain controller whereas lockout events for local accounts are generated on the local computer.

4.8.1 Account Management Event ID Fields

Account activity events contain multiple fields describing what specific action was performed, and by whom. There are certain fields that warrant further explanation. [50] Event ID 4624 consists of six fields on Windows 7: **Subject**, **Logon Type**, **New Logon**, **Process Information**, **Network Information**, and **Detailed Authentication Information**.

The **Subject** field identifies who requested the logon. The **New Logon** and **Network Information** fields provide respective information about the new account logon and the origin of the request. **Process Information** and **Detailed Authentication** is used to identify the process that performed the logon request and the authentication mechanism used.

In event ID 4624, the sub-field **Security ID** of the **Subject** section may have NULL SID as a value. NULL SID is an account identifier (SID: S-1-0-0) used for unknown SID values. [51]

4.9 Kernel Driver Signing

Introduction of kernel driver signing in the 64-bit version of Windows Vista significantly improves defenses against insertion of malicious drivers or activities in the kernel. [52] Any indication of a protected driver being altered may indicate malicious activity or a disk error and warrants investigation.

---

[50] Event ID 4624 provides details of each field at the end of the event.
[51] http://technet.microsoft.com/en-us/library/cc778824(v=ws.10).aspx
[52] http://msdn.microsoft.com/en-us/library/windows/hardware/ff548231(v=vs.85).aspx

	ID	Level	Event Log	Event Source
Detected an invalid image hash of a file	5038	Informational	Security	Microsoft-Windows-Security-Auditing
Detected an invalid page hash of an image file	6281	Informational	Security	Microsoft-Windows-Security-Auditing
Code Integrity Check	3001, 3002, 3003, 3004, 3010, 3023	Warning, Error	Microsoft-Windows-CodeIntegrity/Operational	Microsoft-Windows-CodeIntegrity
Failed Kernel Driver Loading	219	Warning	System	Microsoft-Windows-Kernel-PnP

Table 10: Kernel Driver Signing Events

4.10 Group Policy Errors

Management of domain computers permits administrators to heighten the security and regulation of those machines with Group Policy. The inability to apply a policy due to a group policy error reduces the aforementioned benefits. An administrator should investigate these events immediately.

	ID	Level	Event Log	Event Source
Internal Error	1125	Error	System	Microsoft-Windows-GroupPolicy
Generic Internal Error	1127	Error	System	Microsoft-Windows-GroupPolicy
Group Policy Application Failed due to Connectivity	1129	Error	System	Microsoft-Windows-GroupPolicy

Table 11: Group Policy Errors Events

4.11 Windows Defender Activities

Spyware and malware remain a serious problem and Microsoft developed an antispyware and antivirus, Windows Defender, to combat this threat. [53] Any notifications of detecting, removing, preventing these malicious programs should be investigated. In the event Windows Defender fails to operate normally, administrators should correct the issue immediately to prevent the possibility of infection or further infection. If a third-party antivirus and antispyware product is currently in use, the collection of these events is not necessary.

---

[53] http://windows.microsoft.com/en-us/windows-8/windows-defender

Scan Failed	1005	Error	Microsoft-Windows-Windows Defender/Operational	Microsoft-Windows-Windows Defender
Detected Malware	1006	Warning	Microsoft-Windows-Windows Defender/Operational	Microsoft-Windows-Windows Defender
Action on Malware Failed	1008	Error	Microsoft-Windows-Windows Defender/Operational	Microsoft-Windows-Windows Defender
Failed to remove item from quarantine	1010	Error	Microsoft-Windows-Windows Defender/Operational	Microsoft-Windows-Windows Defender
Failed to update signatures	2001	Error	Microsoft-Windows-Windows Defender/Operational	Microsoft-Windows-Windows Defender
Failed to update engine	2003	Error	Microsoft-Windows-Windows Defender/Operational	Microsoft-Windows-Windows Defender
Reverting to last known good set of signatures	2004	Warning	Microsoft-Windows-Windows Defender/Operational	Microsoft-Windows-Windows Defender
Real-Time Protection failed	3002	Error	Microsoft-Windows-Windows Defender/Operational	Microsoft-Windows-Windows Defender
Unexpected Error	5008	Error	Microsoft-Windows-Windows Defender/Operational	Microsoft-Windows-Windows Defender

Table 12: Windows Defender Activities Events

4.12 Mobile Device Activities

Wireless devices are ubiquitous and the need to record an enterprise's wireless device activities may be critical. A wireless device could become compromised while traveling between different networks, regardless of the protocol used for communication (e.g., 802.11 or Bluetooth). Therefore, the tracking of which networks mobile devices are entering and exiting is useful to prevent further compromises. The creation frequency of the following events depends on how often the device disconnects and reconnects to a wireless network. Each event below provides mostly similar information with the exception that additional fields have been added to certain events.

	ID	Level	Event Log	Event Source
Network Connection and Disconnection Status (Wired and Wireless)	10000,10001	Informational	Microsoft-Windows-NetworkProfile/Operational	Microsoft-Windows-NetworkProfile
Starting a Wireless connection	8000, 8011	Informational	Microsoft-Windows-WLAN-AutoConfig/Operational	Microsoft-Windows-WLAN-AutoConfig
Successfully connected to Wireless connection	8001	Informational	Microsoft-Windows-WLAN-AutoConfig/Operational	Microsoft-Windows-WLAN-AutoConfig
Disconnect from Wireless connection	8003	Informational	Microsoft-Windows-WLAN-AutoConfig/Operational	Microsoft-Windows-WLAN-AutoConfig
Wireless Association Status	11000, 11001, 11002	Informational Error	Microsoft-Windows-WLAN-AutoConfig/Operational	Microsoft-Windows-WLAN-AutoConfig
Wireless Security Started, Stopped, Successful, or Failed	11004, 11005, 11010, 11006	Informational Error	Microsoft-Windows-WLAN-AutoConfig/Operational	Microsoft-Windows-WLAN-AutoConfig
Wireless Connection Failed	8002	Error	Microsoft-Windows-WLAN-AutoConfig/Operational	Microsoft-Windows-WLAN-AutoConfig
Wireless Authentication Started and Failed	12011, 12012 12013	Informational Error	Microsoft-Windows-WLAN-AutoConfig/Operational	Microsoft-Windows-WLAN-AutoConfig

Table 13: Mobility related Events

4.13 External Media Detection

Detection of USB device (e.g., mass storage devices) usage is important in some environments, such as air gapped networks. This section attempts to take the proactive avenue to detect USB insertion at real-time. Event ID 43 only appears under certain circumstances. The following events and event logs are only available in Windows 8 and above. Additional information can be found in the footnotes.

	ID	Level	Event Log	Event Source
New Device Information	43[54]	Informational	Microsoft-Windows-USB-USBHUB3-Analytic[55][56]	Microsoft-Windows-USB-USBHUB3
New Mass Storage Installation	400[57]	Informational	Microsoft-Windows-Kernel-PnP/Device Configuration	Microsoft-Windows-Kernel-PnP
New Mass Storage Installation	410[57]	Informational	Microsoft-Windows-Kernel-PnP/Device Configuration	Microsoft-Windows-Kernel-PnP

Table 14: External Media Detection Events

Microsoft-Windows-USB-USBHUB3-Analytic is not an event log per se; it is a trace session log that stores tracing events in an Event Trace Log (.etl) file. The events created by Microsoft-Windows-USB-USBHUB3 publisher are sent to a direct channel (i.e., Analytic log) and cannot be subscribed too for event collection. [58] Administrators should seek an alternative method of collecting and analyzing this event (43).

---

[54] This event is generated for any USB 2.0 and 3.0 devices being inserted into an USB 3.0 port. The respective event log was not introduced until Windows 8.
[55] This is an **Analytic** log (i.e., this is an Event Tracing for Windows, ETW, trace session log). These logs are disabled by default. When the channel is enabled, ETW will start processing this event.
[56] http://technet.microsoft.com/en-us/library/cc749492.aspx
[57] This event is generated for any USB device being inserted into any USB port (2.0 or 3.0). However, this event is only generated once (the first time the device is introduced into the system).
[58] http://msdn.microsoft.com/en-us/library/aa385225.aspx

4.14 Printing Services

Document printing is essential for daily operations in many environments. The vast amount of printing requests increases the difficulty in tracking and identifying which document was printed and by whom. Documents forwarded to a printer for processing can be recorded for logging purposes in multiple ways. Each printing job can be logged either by a printing server, the printer itself, or the requesting machine. The logging of these activities permits early detection of printing certain documents. The following event is generated on the client machine requesting to print a document. The event listed below may be produced excessively depending on printing activity. This event should be treated as a historical record or an additional piece of evidence rather than an auditing record of printing jobs.

	ID	Level	Event Log	Event Source
Printing Document	307	Informational	Microsoft-Windows-PrintService/Operational	Microsoft-Windows-PrintService

Table 15: Printing Services Events

This operational log is disabled by default and requires the log to be enabled to capture this event.

4.15 Pass the Hash Detection

Tracking user accounts for detecting Pass the Hash (PtH) requires creating a custom view with XML to configure more advanced filtering options. The event query language is based on XPath. The recommended **QueryList** below is limited in detecting PTH attacks. These queries focus on discovering lateral movement by an attacker using local accounts that are not part of the domain. The **QueryList** captures events that show a local account attempting to connect remotely to another machine not part of the domain. This event is a rarity so any occurrence should be treated as suspicious.

These XPath queries below are used for the Event Viewer's **Custom Views**.

The successful use of PtH for lateral movement between workstations would trigger event ID 4624, with an event level of Information, from the security log. This behavior would be a **LogonType** of 3 using NTLM authentication where it is not a domain logon and not the ANONYMOUS LOGON account. To clearly summarize the event that is being collected:

EventID	Log	Level	LogonType	Authentication Package Name
4624	Security	Information	3	NTLM

In the **QueryList** below, substitute the <DOMAIN NAME> section with the desired domain name.

```
<QueryList>
 <Query Id="0" Path="ForwardedEvents">
  <Select Path="ForwardedEvents">
   *[System[(Level=4 or Level=0) and (EventID=4624)]]
   and
   *[EventData[Data[@Name='LogonType'] and (Data='3')]]
   and
   *[EventData[Data[@Name='AuthenticationPackageName'] = 'NTLM']]
   and
   *[EventData[Data[@Name='TargetUserName'] != 'ANONYMOUS LOGON']]
   and
   *[EventData[Data[@Name='TargetDomainName'] != '<DOMAIN NAME>']]
 </Select>
 </Query>
</QueryList>
```

A failed logon attempt when trying to move laterally using PtH would trigger an event ID 4625. This would have a **LogonType** of 3 using NTLM authentication where it is not a domain logon and not the ANONYMOUS LOGON account. To clearly summarize the event that is being collected:

EventID	Log	Level	LogonType	Authentication Package Name
4625	Security	Information	3	NTLM

```
<QueryList>
 <Query Id="0" Path="ForwardedEvents">
  <Select Path="ForwardedEvents">
   *[System[(Level=4 or Level=0) and (EventID=4625)]]
   and
   *[EventData[Data[@Name='LogonType'] and (Data='3')]]
   and
   *[EventData[Data[@Name='AuthenticationPackageName'] = 'NTLM']]
   and
   *[EventData[Data[@Name='TargetUserName'] != 'ANONYMOUS LOGON']]
   and
   *[EventData[Data[@Name='TargetDomainName'] != '<DOMAIN NAME>']]
 </Select>
 </Query>
</QueryList>
```

4.16 Remote Desktop Logon Detection

Remote Desktop account activity events are not easily identifiable using the Event Viewer GUI. When an account remotely connects to a client, a generic successful logon event is created. A custom **Query Filter** can aid in clarifying the type of logon that was performed. The query below shows logins using Remote Desktop. Remote Desktop activity should be monitored since only certain administrators should be using it, and they should be from a limited set of management workstations. Any Remote Desktop logins outside of expected activity should be investigated.

The XPath queries below are used for the Event Viewer's **Custom Views**. Event ID 4624 and Event ID 4634 respectively indicate when a user has logged on and logged off with RDP. A LogonType with the value of 10 indicates a Remote Interactive logon. [59]

---

[59] http://msdn.microsoft.com/en-us/library/windows/desktop/aa380129(v=vs.85).aspx

EventID	Log	Level	LogonType	Authentication Package Name
4624	Security	Information	10	Negotiate
4634	Security	Information	10	N/A

```
<QueryList>
 <Query Id="0" Path="ForwardedEvents">
  <Select Path="ForwardedEvents">
<!-- Collects Logon and Logoffs of RDP -->
<!-- Remote Desktop Protocol Connections -->
    *[System[(Level=4 or Level=0) and (EventID=4624 or EventID=4634)]]
    and
    *[EventData[Data[@Name='LogonType']='10')]]
    and
(*[EventData[Data[5]='10')]]
    or
    *[EventData[Data[@Name='AuthenticationPackageName'] = 'Negotiate']])
</Select>
 </Query>
</QueryList>
```

5   Event Log Retention

It is recommended that the Forwarded Events log file on the server designated as the central point for log collection is set to a size of approximately 1GB and enable the **Archive the log when full, do not overwrite events** policy to control the behavior when the event log has reach capacity. The theoretical maximum log file size for the forwarded events log on Windows Server 2008 R2 is 2 terabytes [60], but as the log file becomes larger the Event Viewer UI takes longer to load and show results for custom views. Depending on the size of the network, a 1GB forwarded events log file can hold anywhere from a few hours to a few days worth of log data. Due to this size limitation, it is important to review the log regularly (once a day) and setup archiving, or alternatively feed the log data into some larger Security Information Event Management (SIEM) system.

It may be beneficial to have the Forwarded Events log file reside on a larger and separate disk. An alternative option is to store the Forwarded Events log file on a network mapped drive that has a large amount of disk space. This slight modification can be completed by:

1. Open Event Viewer
2. Select **Forwarded Events** under **Windows Logs** and right-click **Forwarded Events**
3. Select **Properties**
4. Change **Log Path** to specify the absolute path to new log file
     a.   Network-mapped drives must be specified by their names (e.g., \\NetDrive\newdir\Fwd.evtx)
5. Select **OK**

This modification will not affect custom views or subscriptions already deployed.

---

[60] http://technet.microsoft.com/en-us/library/hh125924(v=ws.10).aspx

Client workstations and servers in DoD should follow the DISA STIG for setting the size of other log files (Application, System, Setup, and Security). [61][62]

The maximum log file sizes are intended for the server whose role is the event collection server of the domain. Client machines do not need to specify a maximum log size or retention policy on log files not mentioned in the DISA STIG. When Event Forwarding is properly configured, all subscribed (collected) events from those logs not mentioned by the DISA STIG will be sent to the collector for archiving.

6   Final Recommendations

The central collection of event information helps enterprises gain significant awareness into activities occurring on the network. Collecting targeted events has the benefit of reducing network and storage requirements while providing useful audit information. Targeted event collection reduces the burden and time required for administrators to review logs which may lead to administrators detecting unapproved or malicious activities.

7   Appendix

PowerShell scripts and subscription XML files associated with this guide can be on found on the IAD GitHub site at https://github.com/iadgov

7.1   Subscriptions

Event Forwarding on Windows uses subscriptions to specify which events from a set of computers to collect. This section discusses the details of subscriptions and custom subscriptions for Windows 7 computers.

The sample subscription files in this section can be copied as XML files and loaded into the event collector using the command line tool, wecutil.exe. Each of the sample subscriptions do not specify whom is permitted to use the subscriptions (**AllowedSourceDomainComputers** is blank). The creation of the sample subscription can be completed by executing the following commands in order:

1. **wecutil cs <xml_file_path>.xml**
    a. An error stating **The subscription fails to activate** will appear so ignore it
2. **wmic path Win32_group where name='EventSource' get sid**
    a. Store this value temporarily
3. Obtain the value of the *SubscriptionId* element from the subscription XML file
4. Using the SID value found in step 2, correct the subscriptions configuration by executing **wecutil ss SubscriptionId /adc:O:NSG:BAD:P(A;;GA;;;sid_value)S:**
5. To verify that no issues are present, execute **wecutil rs SubscriptionId**

The parameter /adc of wecutil is used to set a Security Descriptor Definition Language (SDDL) for the targeted subscription. SDDL is briefly discussed in the Security Descriptor Definition Language section.

---

[61] DISA STIG: Windows 7 Security Technical Implementation Guide Version 1. Group ID (Vulid): V-26579, V-26580, V-26581, V-26582
[62] DISA STIG: Windows Server 2008 R2 Security Technical Implementation Guide Version 1. Group ID (Vulid): V-26579, V-26580, V-26581, V-26582

7.1.1 Subscription XML Details

A subscription is simply a XML file that describes to the operating system what event logs to collect and forward. The following subscription example demonstrates the collection of all events in the Application log from a source (client). The targeted sources are the Domain Computers group and the Domain Controllers group. This subscription example is for testing purposes as it will collect a large amount of events and is not recommended for production use. The example below conforms to the MS-WSMV: Web Services Management Protocol Extensions for Windows Vista, as the subscription was created on Windows Server 2008 R2. [63]

```
<?xml version="1.0" encoding="UTF-8"?>
<Subscription xmlns="http://schemas.microsoft.com/2006/03/windows/events/subscription">
    <SubscriptionId>Application Log</SubscriptionId>
    <SubscriptionType>SourceInitiated</SubscriptionType>
    <Description></Description>
    <Enabled>true</Enabled>
    <Uri>http://schemas.microsoft.com/wbem/wsman/1/windows/EventLog</Uri>
    <ConfigurationMode>MinLatency</ConfigurationMode>
    <Delivery Mode="Push">
        <Batching>
            <MaxLatencyTime>30000</MaxLatencyTime>
        </Batching>
        <PushSettings>
            <Heartbeat Interval="3600000"/>
        </PushSettings>
    </Delivery>
    <Query>
        <![CDATA[
<QueryList><Query Id="0"><Select Path="Application">*[System[(Level=0 or Level=
1 or Level=2 or Level=3 or Level=4 or Level=5)]]</Select></Query></QueryList>
        ]]>
    </Query>
    <ReadExistingEvents>false</ReadExistingEvents>
    <TransportName>HTTP</TransportName>
    <ContentFormat>RenderedText</ContentFormat>
    <Locale Language="en-US"/>
    <LogFile>ForwardedEvents</LogFile>
    <PublisherName>Microsoft-Windows-EventCollector</PublisherName>
    <AllowedSourceNonDomainComputers></AllowedSourceNonDomainComputers>
    <AllowedSourceDomainComputers> O:NSG:NSD (A;;GA;;;DC)(A;;GA;;;DD)</AllowedSourceDomainComputers>
</Subscription>
```

The following table details each node of the above subscription: [63]

---

[63] wecutil ss -?

Node	Description
Subscription	The subscription schema
SubscriptionId	The subscription's identification
Description	Describes the subscription
Enabled	Specifies if the current subscription is enabled or disabled
Uri	The type of event used by the subscription.
ConfigurationMode	Used for the Event Delivery Optimization of subscriptions. The four valid options are: **Normal, MinLatency, MinBandwidth** or **Custom**
Delivery Mode	Indicates how events should be sent to the subscription manager. The mode can either be: **Push** (Source-Initiated) or **Pull** (Collector-Initiated)
QueryList	Used for event filtering and <Select></Select> is a XPath query [64]
Heartbeat	Used to validate the client's connectivity with subscription [65]
ReadExistingEvents	Notifies the subscription to read all events matching the filter [64]
TransportName	Indicates that either HTTP or HTTPS will be used
ContentFormat	Specifies how the event data will be given to the subscription manager [64]
Locale	Language that the response is translated too [64]
LogFile	The event log file where the received events will be stored at
PublisherName	The name of the publisher that owns or imports the log file
AllowedSourceNonDomainComputers	List the allowed non-domain computers that can receive the subscription
AllowedSourceDomainComputers	List the allowed domain computers that can receive the subscription

Table 16: Subscription XML Description

7.1.2   Sample Subscriptions to Collect Recommended Events

Sample subscriptions provided in conjunction with this security guidance can be found in Subscriptions\NT6 and Subscriptions\samples directories of the EvtFwdSubscriptions_r.zip ZIP file. This compressed file consists of scripts and subscriptions to automate the use of Event Collection. These subscriptions collect the recommended events discussed in the Recommended Events to Collect section of this guide. These subscriptions targets event collected from Windows 7 and above workstations.

7.2   Event ID Definitions

This guidance document has given a list of event IDs to be aware of when monitoring activity. This list is not complete nor should it be the only set of events to be collected. Each environment will most likely focus on specific events or currently using a third party application for event monitoring.

Microsoft's Events and Errors Message Center web site provides a central location for identifying some event IDs for each Windows operating system. [66] Effective use of this resource requires an event ID, or some other information about the event, is known beforehand.

Windows Server 2003 auditing event ID listings can be found in two locations [67]
- Auditing Policy from Windows Server 2003: Security and Protection:
  http://technet.microsoft.com/en-us/library/cc779526(v=ws.10).aspx
- Chapter 4 of the Windows Server 2003 Security Guide:
  http://technet.micosoft.com/library/cc163121.aspx

Windows Server 2008 and Windows Server 2008 R2 events and errors details for general OS components can be found on Microsoft's TechNet website
- Windows Server 2008: Events and Errors
  http://technet.microsoft.com/en-us/library/cc754424(v=ws.10).aspx

---

[64] ([MS-WSMV]: Web Services Management Protocol Extensions for Windows Vista, 2012)
[65] (Web Services Management - WS-MAN, 2008)
[66] http://www.microsoft.com/technet/support/ee/ee_advanced.aspx
[67] http://blogs.msdn.com/b/ericfitz/archive/2007/10/12/list-of-windows-server-2003-events.aspx

Windows Server 2008 Component-Based Servicing events
- Update and package related events:
  http://technet.microsoft.com/en-us/library/cc756291(v=ws.10).aspx

Windows 7 and above AppLocker Event IDs and definitions:
- http://technet.microsoft.com/en-us/library/ee844150(v=ws.10).aspx

Windows Vista, Windows Server 2008, Windows 7 and Windows Server 2008 R2 security audit events are provided by Microsoft either by a support article or a downloadable Excel file. [68][69][70] The Windows operating system, beginning with Windows Vista, provides a command line tool, wevtutil, to list all event IDs raised by a publisher along with the event's message. [71]

The Windows Events Command Line Utility can obtain information regarding event logs and publishers. [72] The following command will get the publisher (gp/get-publisher), obtain information on events that the publisher uses, and produce readable messages for each event. This command can be applied to any publisher to obtain a list of all their events.

wevtutil gp Microsoft-Windows-Security-Auditing /ge:true /gm:true[73]

The mapping of security event IDs between Windows XP and the latest versions of Windows can be revealed in some cases by a simple addition or subtraction of $4096_{10}/0x1000_{16}$. [74] This rule is not applicable to events dealing with successful and failed logons. [74]

7.3   Windows Remote Management Versions
There have been five versions of WinRM since its introduction in Windows Server 2003 R2 as of this writing. The following table correlates each WinRM version to a supported Windows operating system version. [75]

---

[68] http://www.microsoft.com/en-us/download/details.aspx?id=17871

[69] http://support.microsoft.com/kb/947226

[70] http://www.micrsoft.com/en-us/download/details.aspx?id=21561

[71] wevtutil /?

[72] http://technet.microsoft.com/en-us/library/cc732848(WS.10).aspx

[73] http://blogs.microsoft.com/b/ericfitz/archive/2007/07/31/documentation-on-the-windows-vista-and-windows-server-2008-security-events.aspx

[74] http://blogs.msdn.com/b/ericfitz/archive/2009/06/10/mapping-pre-vista-security-events-ids-to-security-events-ids-in-vista.aspx

[75] http://technet.microsoft.com/en-us/library/ff520073(v=ws.10).aspx

Version	Support
WinRM 0.5	Windows Server 2003 R2*
WinRM 1.0	Windows Vista
WinRM 1.1	Windows Vista SP1 Windows Server 2008 Windows Server 2003 SP1** Windows Server 2003 SP2** Windows Server 2003 R2** Windows XP SP2**
WinRM 2.0	Windows 7 Windows Server 2008 R2 Windows Server 2008 SP1*** Windows Server 2008 SP2*** Windows Vista SP1*** Windows Vista SP2*** Windows XP SP3***
WinRM 3.0	Windows 8 Windows 7 SP1**** Windows Server 2008 SP1**** Windows Server 2008 SP2****

Table 17: WinRM Version Correlation

* = Installed from the Add/Remove System Components feature within the Hardware Management feature

** = Install WS-Management v1.1. [76]

*** = Installed as part of the Windows Management Framework Core package. [77][78] This update requires at least Microsoft .NET Framework 2.0 Service Pack 1. [79]

**** = Installed as part of Windows Management Framework 3.0. This update requires at least Microsoft .NET Framework 4.0. [80]

Installation packages for WinRM can be found in knowledge base articles, shown below.

WinRM Version (KB#)	Supported OS	KB URIs
WinRM 1.1 (KB936059)	Windows Server 2003 SP1 Windows Server 2003 SP2 Windows XP SP2 Windows XP SP3*	http://support.microsoft.com/kb/936059 +
WinRM 2.0 (KB968930)	Windows Server 2003 SP2 Windows Server 2008 Windows Server 2008 SP2 Windows Vista SP1 Windows Vista SP2 Windows XP SP2* Windows XP SP3	http://support.microsoft.com/kb/968930 + * Requires Microsoft Windows Installer 3.1 * Requires .NET Framework 2.0 SP1
WinRM 3.0 (KB2506146)	Windows 7 SP1 Windows Server 2008 R2 SP1 Windows Server 2008 SP2	http://support.microsoft.com/kb/2506146 + * Requires .NET Framework 4.0 * Update comes with Release Notes

Table 18: WinRM Version Update URLs

Microsoft published a knowledge base article (KB936059)[81] and an update for WinRM 1.1. [82] The knowledge base article offers additional post-installation information to the update that is not mentioned in this document. The actual update can be applied to Windows XP SP2, Windows Server 2003 SP1, Windows Server 2003 SP2, and Windows 2003 Server R2.

---

[76] https://www.microsoft.com/en-us/download/details.aspx?id=21900

[77] https://www.microsoft.com/en-us/download/details.aspx?id=9864

[78] https://www.microsoft.com/en-us/download/details.aspx?id=16818

[79] https://www.microsoft.com/en-us/download/details.aspx?id=16614

[80] https://www.microsoft.com/en-us/download/details.aspx?id=34595

[81] http://support.microsoft.com/kb/936059

[82] https://www.microsoft.com/en-us/download/details.aspx?id=21900

7.4 WinRM 2.0 Configuration Settings

The quick configuration option of WinRM uses the following default configuration settings on Windows Server 2008 R2. [21][83] Default values of WinRM configuration settings are shown and referenced from Microsoft Developer Network (MSDN) in this document for convenience. [21] The following WinRM command displays the configuration setting of WinRM

winrm get winrm/config

It produces the following example output:

```
Config
    MaxEnvelopeSizekb = 150
    MaxTimeoutms = 60000
    MaxBatchItems = 32000
    MaxProviderRequests = 4294967295
    Client
        NetworkDelayms = 5000
        URLPrefix = wsman
        AllowUnencrypted = false
        Auth
            Basic = true
            Digest = true
            Kerberos = true
            Negotiate = true
            Certificate = true
            CredSSP = false
        DefaultPorts
            HTTP = 5985
            HTTPS = 5986
        TrustedHosts
    Service
        RootSDDL = O NSG:BAD:P(A;;GA;;;BA)S P(AU;FA;GA;;;WD)(AU;SA;GWGX;;;WD)
        MaxConcurrentOperations = 4294967295
        MaxConcurrentOperationsPerUser = 15
        EnumerationTimeoutms = 60000
        MaxConnections = 25
        MaxPacketRetrievalTimeSeconds = 120
        AllowUnencrypted = false
        Auth
            Basic = false
            Kerberos = true
            Negotiate = true
            Certificate = false
            CredSSP = false
            CbtHardeningLevel = Relaxed
        DefaultPorts
            HTTP = 5985
            HTTPS = 5986
        IPv4Filter = *
        IPv6Filter = *
        EnableCompatibilityHttpListener = false
        EnableCompatibilityHttpsListener = false
        CertificateThumbprint
    Winrs
        AllowRemoteShellAccess = true
        IdleTimeout = 180000
        MaxConcurrentUsers = 5
        MaxShellRunTime = 2147483647
        MaxProcessesPerShell = 15
        MaxMemoryPerShellMB = 150
        MaxShellsPerUser = 5
```

Each of field of the above output is described in the following sections.

7.4.1 Protocol Settings

These settings are configurable options for the WS-Management protocol used by WinRM.

---

[83] ([MS-WSMV]: Web Services Management Protocol Extensions for Windows Vista, 2012)

Parameters	Description
MaxEnvelopeSizekb	The Simple Object Access Protocol (SOAP) data size has maximum in kilobytes **Default is 150 kilobytes**
MaxTimeoutms	Each push request (not pull) has a maximum timeout. This value is in milliseconds. **Default is 60000ms (60 seconds)**
MaxBatchItems	The limit of elements used in a pull response. **Default for WinRM 1.1 and earlier: 20** **Default for WinRM 2.0: 32000**
MaxProviderRequests	The limit on concurrent requests. **Default for WinRM 1.1 and earlier: 25** **Default for WinRM 2.0: Unsupported/Undefined**

Table 19: Protocol Settings

7.4.2 Client Configuration

The following parameters configures on how the WinRM client operates.

Parameters	Description
NetworkDelayms	A time buffer for the client computer to wait in milliseconds. **Default WinRM 1.1 and earlier: 5000** **Default WinRM 2.0: 5000**
URLPrefix	The type of URLPrefix used on request for HTTP or HTTPS requests. **Default WinRM 1.1 and earlier: wsman** **Default WinRM 2.0: wsman**
AllowUnencrypted	Clients are allowed to request unencrypted traffic. **Default WinRM 1.1 and earlier: false** **Default WinRM 2.0: false**
Auth	Specifies which authentication method is allowed for the client computer
DefaultPorts	**Default WinRM 1.1 and earlier: HTTP = 80, HTTPS = 443** **Default WinRM 2.0: HTTP = 5985, HTTPS = 5986**
TrustedHosts	These trusted hosts do not need to be authenticated.

Table 20: WinRM Client Configuration

7.4.3 WinRM Service

The following parameters are used by the WinRM service.

Parameters	Description
RootSDDL	The security descriptor for remotely accessing the listener **Default WinRM 1.1 and earlier:** O:NSG:BAD:P(A;;GA;;;BA)S:P(AU;FA;GA;;;WD)(AU;SA;GWGX;;;WD) **Default WinRM 2.0:** O:NSG:BAD:P(A;;GA;;;BA)(A;;GR;;;ER)S:P(AU;FA;GA;;;WD)
MaxConcurrentOperations	The maximum number of concurrent operations. **Default WinRM 1.1 and earlier: 100** **Default WinRM 2.0: replaced with MaxConcurrentOperationPerUser**
MaxConcurrentOperationsPerUser	The limit of concurrent operation for each user on the same system. **Default WinRM 1.1 and earlier: Not available** **Default WinRM 2.0: 15**
EnumerationTimeoutms	The idle timeout between pull messages in milliseconds. **Default WinRM 1.1 and earlier: 60000** **Default WinRM 2.0: 60000**
MaxConnections	The maximum number of simultaneous active requests that can be processed. **Default WinRM 1.1 and earlier: 5** **Default WinRM 2.0: 25**
MaxPacketRetrievalTimeSeconds	The limit on the number of seconds to retrieve a packet. **Default WinRM 1.1 and earlier: Not available** **Default WinRM 2.0: 120**
AllowUnencrypted	Clients are allowed to request unencrypted traffic. **Default WinRM 1.1 and earlier: false** **Default WinRM 2.0: false**
Auth	Specifies which authentication method is allowed for the client computer.
DefaultPorts	**Default WinRM 1.1 and earlier: HTTP = 80, HTTPS = 443** **Default WinRM 2.0: HTTP = 5985, HTTPS = 5986**
IPv(4/6) Filter	The IP for the WinRM service to listen on. **Default WinRM 1.1 and earlier: Any** **Default WinRM 2.0: Any**
EnableCompatibilityHttpListener	Service listens on port 80 and port 5985. **WinRM 1.1 and earlier: Not supported**
EnableCompatibilityHttpsListener	Service listens on port 443 and port 5986. **WinRM 1.1 and earlier: Not supported**
CertificateThumbprint	The certificate thumb print used for https. **WinRM 1.1 and earlier: Not supported**

Table 21: WinRM Service

7.4.4 WinRS

Windows Remote Shell (WinRS) is turned on by default. The recommendation is to disable it. Each of the parameters for WinRS will use the default value if no policy is configured. [84][21]

---

[84] http://msdn.microsoft.com/en-us/library/windows/desktop/ee309367(v=vs.85).aspx

Parameters	Description
AllowRemoteShellAccess	Permit remote shell access
IdleTimeout	The time, in milliseconds, before a shell connection is terminated.
MaxConcurrentUsers	Maximum number of users that can request shell access at one time
MaxShellRunTime	Maximum duration, in milliseconds, that command can run for. This value is not configurable in WinRM 2.0.
MaxProcessesPerShell	Maximum number of processes that a single shell can create.
MaxMemoryPerShellMB	Maximum number of memory that a single shell can use.
MaxShellsPerUser	Maximum number of shells a user can create.

Table 22: WinRS Configuration Settings

7.5 WinRM Registry Keys and Values

Throughout this document, registry keys can be used for verification purposes only. Do not to modify any registry keys as this may cause unforeseen problems and possible system corruption. The following registry keys appear once a Domain Controller configures WinRM via Group Policies.

Registry Values	Description
HKLM\SOFTWARE\Policies\Microsoft\Windows\EventLog\EventForwarding\SubscriptionManager\1	Subscription Manager registry key
HKLM\SOFTWARE\Policies\Microsoft\Windows\WinRM\Service\AllowConfig	WinRM Service registry keys
HKLM\SOFTWARE\Policies\Microsoft\Windows\WinRM\Service\IPv4Filter	
HKLM\SOFTWARE\Policies\Microsoft\Windows\WinRM\Service\IPv6Filter	
HKLM\SOFTWARE\Policies\Microsoft\Windows\WinRM\Service\AllowBasic	
HKLM\SOFTWARE\Policies\Microsoft\Windows\WinRM\Service\AllowUnencryptedTraffic	
HKLM\SOFTWARE\Policies\Microsoft\Windows\WinRM\Service\AllowCredSSP	
HKLM\SOFTWARE\Policies\Microsoft\Windows\WinRM\Service\AllowKerberos	
HKLM\SOFTWARE\Policies\Microsoft\Windows\WinRM\Service\CBTHardeningLevelStatus	
HKLM\SOFTWARE\Policies\Microsoft\Windows\WinRM\Service\CbtHardeningLevel	
HKLM\SOFTWARE\Policies\Microsoft\Windows\WinRM\Service\AllowNegotiate	
HKLM\SOFTWARE\Policies\Microsoft\Windows\WinRM\Client\AllowBasic	WinRM Client registry keys
HKLM \SOFTWARE\Policies\Microsoft\Windows\WinRM\Client\AllowUnencryptedTraffic	
HKLM \SOFTWARE\Policies\Microsoft\Windows\WinRM\Client\AllowCredSSP	
HKLM \SOFTWARE\Policies\Microsoft\Windows\WinRM\Client\AllowDigest	
HKLM \SOFTWARE\Policies\Microsoft\Windows\WinRM\Client\AllowKerberos	
HKLM \SOFTWARE\Policies\Microsoft\Windows\WinRM\Client\AllowNegotiate	
HKLM\SOFTWARE\Policies\Microsoft\Windows\WinRM\Service\WinRS\AllowRemoteShellAccess	Windows Remote Shell registry keys
HKLM\SOFTWARE\Microsoft\Windows\CurrentVersion\WSMAN\WINRS	
HKLM\SOFTWARE\Microsoft\Windows\CurrentVersion\WSMAN\WINRS\CustomRemoteShell	
HKLM\SOFTWARE\Microsoft\Windows\CurrentVersion\WSMAN\CertMap	WSMAN Services registry keys
HKLM\SOFTWARE\Microsoft\Windows\CurrentVersion\WSMAN\Client	
HKLM\SOFTWARE\Microsoft\Windows\CurrentVersion\WSMAN\Listener	
HKLM\SOFTWARE\Microsoft\Windows\CurrentVersion\WSMAN\Listener*+HTTP	
HKLM\SOFTWARE\Microsoft\Windows\CurrentVersion\WSMAN\Plugin	
HKLM\SOFTWARE\Microsoft\Windows\CurrentVersion\WSMAN\Plugin\EventForwarding Plugin	
HKLM\SOFTWARE\Microsoft\Windows\CurrentVersion\WSMAN\Service	

Table 23: WinRM, WinRS, WSMAN and Event Forwarding Registry Values

7.5.1 Security Descriptor Definition Language

The language in the **AllowedSourceDomainComputers** node is called Security Descriptor Definition Language (SDDL). [85] A subscription can be customized to target single or multiple users, computers, or groups. The SID value of any of the aforementioned entities can be used to configure the targeted subscription's SDDL.

---

[85] http://msdn.micosoft.com/en-us/library/windows/desktop/aa379567(v=vs.85).aspx

Microsoft provided the SDDL structure as shown: [86]

O: Owner_SID
G: Group_SID
D: DACL_FLAGS(string_ace1)(string_ace2)…. (string_aceN)
S: SACL_FLAGS(string_ace1)(string_ace2)…. (string_aceN)

string_ace are optional Access Control Entries.

ACE has the following structure: [87]
(AceType;AceFlags;Rights;ObjectGuid;InheritObjectGuid;AccountSID;resource_attribute)

There is also an option to use conditional ACE; however, that will not be discussed here. [88]

An example of a SDDL is:
O:NSG:NSD:(A;;GA;;;DC)(A;;GA;;;NS)

The breakdown of **O:NSG:NSD:** is shown:

SID and Flags	Description
O:	Network Service
G:	Network Service
D:	None

String_ACE breakdown of (A;;GA;;;DC) (A;;GA;;;NS)

String ACE1	String ACE2
(A;;GA;;;DC)	(A;;GA;;;NS)
AceType = "A" = ACCESS_ALLOWED_ACE_TYPE	AceType = "A" = ACCESS_ALLOWED_ACE_TYPE
AceFlags = None	AceFlags = None
Rights = "GA" = GENERIC_ALL	Rights = "GA" = GENERIC_ALL
ObjectGuid = None	ObjectGuid = None
InheritObjectGuid = None	InheritObjectGuid = None
AccountSID = "DC" = Domain Computer	AccoutSID = "NS" = Network Service

7.6 Troubleshooting

Issues may arise such as communication errors between the collectors and sources, authentication errors, and subscriptions errors. WinRM issues can be investigated using certain command line options. Demystifying WinRM's capabilities and behaviors can be achieved by using the help option of WinRM. [89] If any troubleshooting is to be performed while enforcing the authentication recommendations of this guide, then append the –remote:TARGET option to the winrm command. The TARGET should be the local hostname if the issue involves the local machine.

The listing below is not an exhaustive list to identify all issues with WinRM. These commands are helpful to diagnose common errors. [90][91][92]

---

[86] http://msdn.microsoft.com/en-us/library/aa379570(v=vs.85).aspx
[87] http://msdn.microsoft.com/en-us/library/aa374928(v=vs.85).aspx
[88] For curious readers, more information can be found at: http://msdn.microsoft.com/en-us/library/dd981030.aspx.
[89] winrm help
[90] http://blogs.technet.com/b/jonjor/archive/2009/01/09/winrm-windows-remote-management-troubleshooting.aspx

winrm e winrm/config/listener

WinRM can enumerate all listeners that WinRM is currently using.

winrm id –remote:TARGET

This command identifies (id) the remote machine (TARGET) by asking the remote machine its operating system version and WinRM version. The TARGET can be a NetBIOS name, Domain name, or FQDN. Alternatively, using the –auth:none option will force WinRM to not use authentication when requesting information from the remote machine. Using this option only provides a minimal set of details (version of WinRM only).

The identify option provide insight if communication between two WinRM parties are correct and not interrupted. This interruption can be the result of a firewall blocking WinRM or WinRM not running.

winrm get wmi/root/cimv2/Win32_Service?Name=WinRM

This command provides useful information (e.g., ProcessID and Context WinRM runs in) regarding the WinRM service running on the local machine.

winrm invoke restore winrm/config @{}

WinRM allows the restoration of default settings using the previous command.

winrm get winrm/config/client/auth
winrm get winrm/config/service/auth

These two commands display the configuration for both WinRM client and service. Viewing configuration settings can help identify any possible incorrect configuration settings.

winrm helpmsg ERRORCODE

WinRM error messages display the description of the error and an error code. The definition behind the error code can be shown by executing the below command. The ERRORCODE needs to be supplied verbatim as it was displayed in the original error message (e.g., 0x80070005 means Access Denied). These errors are Win32 error codes.

winrm help auth

---

[91] http://msdn.microsoft.com/en-us/library/windows/desktop/ee309364(v=vs.85).aspx
[92] http://msdn.microsoft.com/en-us/library/windows/desktop/aa384295(v=vs.85).aspx#enabling_auth_options

Generally, WinRM produces an error message when authentication fails. The service provides a second option to help the authentication process. A detailed explanation of different authentication methods used by WinRM can be viewed using the above command.

The recommended method to satisfy WinRM is to supply the –remote option with the target hostname (local or remote). If the source is part of a domain, then executing this command requires an uninterrupted connection to the Domain Controller.

Assume the command is being executed on a computer whose hostname is ABCD.
> **winrm get winrm/config –remote:ABCD**

7.6.1 Operational Logs
While troubleshooting an issue, it is natural for one to look at the logs to help to identify a problem. Event Forwarding and WinRM have operational logs that can be viewed in the Event Viewer or by using the command line tool wevtutil.exe.

The operational log files for the Event Collector, Event Forwarding, and WinRM services can be found by navigating to **Applications and Services Logs** in the Event Viewer on Windows Vista and later. The list below shows the location of the operational logs under **Applications and Services Logs**:

- **Microsoft > Windows > EventCollector > Operational**
- **Microsoft > Windows > Eventlog-ForwardPlugin > Operational**
- **Microsoft > Windows > Windows Remote Management > Operational**

The **Eventlog-ForwardPlugin** and **Windows Remote Management** operational logs are the locations that the local WinRM service will log to. Querying the Event Forwarding log can be done by using the **Microsoft-Windows-Forwarding** publisher with the command line tool wevtutil. An example of using wevtutil:
> **wevtutil qe "LOGFILE/CHANNEL" /c:1 /rd:true /q:"XPATH_QUERY"**

If LOGFILE is not within %SYSTEMROOT%\system32\Winevt\Logs, the /lf option must be used with the true argument.

The help documentation of the wevutil tool provides more insight of the other capabilities of the tool. This documentation can be found by executing the following command:

> **wevutil /?**

7.6.2 WinRM Errors
There are numerous errors that WinRM can generate. Microsoft provides a table to easily identify common errors and solutions related to WinRM. [93] A list of event IDs associated with WinRM that applies to Windows Vista and above can be found on Microsoft's TechNet site. [18]

7.6.2.1 Creation of Subscription Errors
Numerous errors could arise during subscription creation: Common errors include

---

[93] http://social.technet.microsoft.com/wiki/contents/articles/13444.windows-server-2012-server-manager-troubleshooting-guide-part-ii-troubleshoot-manageability-status-errors-in-server-manager.aspx#Troubleshoot_manageablility_status_errors

wecutil cs Subscriptions\Logons.xml

One possible error message:
The subscription is saved successfully, but it can't be activated at this time. Use retry-subscription command to retry the subscription. If subscription is running, you can also use get-subscriptionruntimestatus command to get extended error status.
Error = 0x3ae8.
The subscription fails to activate.

This error may be caused by the WinRM Firewall exception rule being disabled. The error code that is displayed is a Win32 error code. The error code's message is shown beneath it.

Another possible error message:
Failed to open subscription. Error = 0x6b5.
The interface is unknown.

This error may be caused by the Windows Event Collector not running.

Sources will create subscriptions locally after receiving a list of subscriptions applicable to them. Certain subscriptions may not be created on the sources due to permissions issues or non-existing logs. WinRM will raise an Event ID 102 with a Win32 error code of 500410 in the **Eventlog-ForwardingPlugin/Operational log**. The error code states that a cluster resource is not available. [94] This error code may be a result of the subscription attempting to access a log file that it does not permissions to access.

Verify the channel's (log file) permissions by navigating to **HKEY_LOCAL_MACHINE\SOFTWARE\Microsoft\Windows\CurrentVersion\WINEVT\Channels** and locating the channel of interest. Within the registry key of the desired channel, view the contents of the registry value named **ChannelAccess** to identify the permissions of the channel. This previous error is applicable to Windows Vista and later.

7.6.2.2 Access Denied Errors
Certain operations of the WinRM command may result in access denied errors. These include:

WSManFault
  Message = Access is denied.

Error number: -2147024891 0x80070005
Access is denied.

- User needs to be part of local administration group, **WinRMRemoteWMIUsers__**, or domain administrator [95][96]
- The administrator password cannot be blank
- Incorrect username or password
- WMI operations need permissions to allow secure connections [97]

---

[94] ([MS-ERREF]: Windows Error Codes)
[95] http://msdn.microsoft.com/en-us/library/aa384295(v=vs.85).aspx
[96] WinRMRemoteWMIUsers__ is a new group in Windows 8 and above

- Windows Firewall service needs to be running

7.6.3   XPath Query Diagnostic

XPath queries used in subscriptions do not display errors to the user who created them when deployed to sources. Query errors are shown in the **Applications and Services Logs > Microsoft > Windows > Eventlog-ForwardingPlugin > Operational** log on Windows Vista and later sources. Event ID 101 raised by the Event Forwarding plug-in is to notify the user an XPath query was incorrect as shown in the following table:

ID	Level	Event Log	Event Source	Operating System Version
101	Warning (3)	Eventlog-ForwardingPlugin/Operational	Eventlog-ForwardingPlugin	Windows Vista+

Table 24: XPath Errors based on OS Version

The human-readable details of the event do not clearly indicate the reason why the event was raised. The specific reason can be identified by viewing the XML details of the event. An error code of the XPath query is hidden as part of the event data. The error code can be viewed by:

1. Locating event ID 101 under the **Eventlog-ForwardingPlugin > Operational** log
2. Selecting the **Details** tab followed by selecting the **XML** view
3. Under the EventData node exists a Data node named **Status** that shows the decimal value of a Win32 error code.

A Win32 error code of 15001 indicates an invalid query of ERROR_EVT_INVALID_QUERY. [98]

8   Works Cited

Distributed Management Task Force, Inc. (2008, 02 12). *Web Services Management - WS-MAN.* Retrieved 10 01, 2012, from Distributed Management Task Force, Inc.: http://www.dmtf.org/standards/published_documents/DSP0226_1.0.0.pdf

Microsoft Corporation. (2012, 07 12). *[MS-CSSP]: Credential Security Support Provider (CredSSP) Procotol.* Retrieved 10 01, 2012, from Microsoft MSDN: http://msdn.microsoft.com/en-us/library/cc226764(v=prot.20).aspx

Microsoft Corporation. (2012, 07 15). *[MS-ERREF]: Windows Error Codes.* Retrieved 10 01, 2012, from Microsoft MSDN: http://msdn.microsoft.com/en-us/library/cc231196.aspx

Microsoft Corporation. (2012, 07 05). *[MS-WSMV]: Web Services Management Protocol Extensions for Windows Vista.* Retrieved 10 01, 2012, from Microsoft MSDN: http://msdn.microsoft.com/en-us/library/cc251526(prot.20).aspx

Microsoft Corporation. (2011, 10 08). *An update is available for the Windows Remote Management feature in Windows Server 2003 and in Windows XP.* Retrieved 10 01, 2012, from Microsoft Support: http://support.microsoft.com/kb/KB936059

Microsoft Corporation. (2012, 10 08). *Installation and Configuration for Windows Remote Management.* Retrieved 10 01, 2012, from Microsoft MSDN: http://msdn.microsoft.com/en-us/library/windows/desktop/aa384372.aspx

Microsoft Corporation. (2012, 10 16). *Setting up a Source Initiated Subscription.* Retrieved 10 01, 2012, from Microsoft MSDN: http://msdn.microsoft.com/en-us/library/bb870973(VS.85).aspx

---

[97] http://msdn.microsoft.com/en-us/library/aa384424(v=vs.85).aspx
[98] http://msdn.microsoft.com/en-us/library/windows/desktop/ms681384(v=vs.84).aspx